Remembering Perfection

Everyday Inspiration
for Living your Spirituality.

Jessica McGregor Johnson

Illustrations by Beatrice Buchser

Remembering Perfection First published in 2008 by;
Ecademy Press
6, Woodland Rise, Penryn, Cornwall, UK. TR10 8QD
info@ecademy-press.com
www.ecademy-press.com

Printed and Bound by; Lightning Source in the UK and USA

Printed on acid-free paper from managed forests. This book is printed on demand, so no copies will be remaindered or pulped.

ISBN 978-1-905823-45-1

The right of Jessica McGregor Johnson to be identified as the author of this work has been asserted in accordance with sections 77 and 78 of the Copyright Designs and Patents Act 1988.

A CIP catalogue record for this book is available from the British Library.

All rights reserved. No part of this work may be reproduced in any material form (including photocopying or storing in any medium by electronic means and whether or not transiently or incidentally to some other use of this publication) without the written permission of the copyright holder except in accordance with the provisions of the Copyright, Designs and Patents Act 1988. Applications for the Copyright holders written permission to reproduce any part of this publication should be addressed to the publishers.

Please note that the information in this book is to inspire you to make the changes you wish for in your life and come back towards wholeness. Any advice or suggestions given are not in any way intended to be authoritative and must be checked out with any relevant qualified professionals before action is taken. This particularly (but not exclusively) applies to any legal, financial or medical decisions you may make.

Copyright © 2008 Jessica McGregor Johnson

For Beatrice

Acknowledgements

Firstly, a deep gratitude to Gurumayi Chidvilasananda, Baba Muktananda and Bhagawan Nityananda, for not only being the light along the path, but also the journey and the goal too. Without their wisdom, teachings, love and example this book would never have been conceivable, let alone written.

To Beatrice, thank you for the wonderful illustrations and design, for being an integral part of the journey, a great supporter and for all the encouragement along the way.

To Hannah Davis, thank you for your professionalism in guiding me through the process of turning 80 pages of rambling thoughts into what is printed here now. Thanks too for being tough on annihilating the paragraph-long sentences I used to favour, and for helping me to develop my personal writing style.

To all at Ecademy Press for their contribution in the production of the book and a special thanks to Mindy Gibbins-Klein for that magic hour when the title came to light.

To all the wonderful people whose lives I have come into contact with, either through family, friendship or work, you gave me such rich experiences, grist for the mill, and thus the content to pass on what I have learnt along the way.

And, thanks to you for buying, reading and using this book, that's definitely worth acknowledging.

CONTENTS

11	**Preface**
17	**Introduction**

CHAPTER ONE
25	**Gratitude**
28	Gratitude in Friendship
31	Gratitude as a Practise
33	Be Grateful for Everything – the Good and the Bad
37	Gratitude for the Lessons in Life
40	Gratitude and Grace

CHAPTER TWO
45	**See God in Each Other**
49	Practising Seeing God in Each Other
51	Compassion Helps
52	Send Blessings, Drop Judgement
54	Forgiveness
59	Asking for Help

CHAPTER THREE
67	**Being Real**
68	Being Real with Ourselves
72	Being Real with Others
75	Being Real in a High Achiever's Business World
79	Being Real, Being Inspired
82	Being Real Energetically

CHAPTER FOUR
93	**Creating Reality**
94	The Energy of Creation
101	Beliefs; Conscious and Subconscious
108	Unearthing the Saboteur
117	The Power of Intention and Visualisation

CHAPTER FIVE
127 Reality and Attitude
131 Being Present in Our Reality
135 The Relationship between Creating Reality and Fear

CHAPTER SIX
149 Unconditional Love
150 What is Unconditional Love?
154 Unconditional Love in Relationships

CHAPTER SEVEN
165 Practising Unconditional Love
171 Love Yourself Physically
173 Loving Yourself Emotionally
176 Loving your Mind
179 Loving your Self

CHAPTER EIGHT
185 Intuition
187 Who is Intuitive?
191 How can we use Intuition in our Lives?
195 Intuition and Self-Esteem

CHAPTER NINE
207 Trust and Faith
208 What is Trust and Faith?
213 Who, What to Trust?
215 Learning to Trust and Have Faith
221 Faith and Prayer

CHAPTER TEN
229 Patience and Surrender
230 Patience is a Virtue
236 What is Surrender?
240 Surrender to Destiny
242 Surrender to our Spiritual Life

CHAPTER ELEVEN
249 What Now?

259 Bibliography and Additional Recommendations

261 Glossary

267 About the Author

Preface

*A personal journey to the eye of the storm.
The calm centre.*

Before I stumbled across the idea of living with a spiritual focus, I never really looked at life. I hadn't contemplated who I was, what life was for, what was going on or how I could influence my experience of it. Life just happened, storms came along and I weathered them as best I could. I would bemoan my fate to whomever would listen and blamed whomever I could. The idea of taking responsibility for my life never occurred to me. My version of feeling alive was jumping off a hill with a hang-glider strapped to my back and in some ways that was my spiritual substitute. I lived life on the surface, not even knowing that there was another level.

In my early thirties things started to change. My marriage had ended and I was in counselling, trying to figure out what direction to go in and how to get 'back on track'. My counsellor recommended a personal development course, "maybe it will help you get in touch with your anger," she said. On the first night I freaked out. I was being asked to let go of the control with which I had governed my life. To drop the barriers, allow others in. I realised I would have to let people see me for the first time, warts and all. I saw that I was being challenged to drop the mask I had worn so tightly; the one that I thought made me socially acceptable. I was out the door. However, they persuaded me to stay, something inside of me so longed for the freedom they were offering and it was the best thing I could have done. I called my counsellor on the Monday – my opening words were, "On Friday night I hated you – by Sunday I loved you!"

For many reasons, this course was a starting point for me. During the weekend I can remember sitting there and feeling excited at what I was hearing. At one point the facilitator was speaking about belief systems. As he said the words 'you are God' in the middle of a sentence, he was looking directly at me. I can't remember exactly what he was talking about or what he meant, but at that moment our eyes linked. He then carried on with his talk but I heard not a word. Those three words had gone straight into me; they hit somewhere very deep and resonated as truth. Up until that moment I hadn't thought much about God for probably over twenty years but as I sat in this seminar I knew without a doubt – of course I am! I didn't have the faintest idea what this meant but I knew one thing for sure – I just knew that this life as I lived it couldn't be all there was, there had to be something more. My spiritual search began.

And it is quite a journey. I can see that I have veered off the normal society/cultural path. I have chosen to live my life differently with a focus not always understood by others. On the whole, our culture calls for us to succeed materially, and all else comes second. I now believe that material success is not the be-all and end-all and, equally important, is the awareness with which we live our lives. This belief has been maturing over the past fifteen years and the living of it is still a work in process.

My journey started normally enough, a career in sales that matured to management, recruitment and training. I was married, and by my late twenties had attained most of the material things that I believed would make me happy. I even had the thatched cottage with the roses over the door. But there was something missing and after my marriage ended I started to search for that elusive 'something'. My search took me to many different places. On leaving the corporate world I went to run a retreat centre in Dorset. It was my first foray into the alternative healing world and I saw how people arrived looking grey and worn out and left with a sparkle in their eyes and a renewed zest for life. Many synchronistic events later found me in the Gurudev Siddha Peeth ashram in Ganeshpuri, India in February 1994. I had finally found that 'something', an ancient teaching that ran true deep within me. After three life-changing months, I returned and gave myself nine months off in Southern Ireland to reassess my life.

In 1997, after three years meeting and working with a wide variety of people at an environmental agency in London, I decided it was time to move on and I made plans to go and live in

Ireland, a place close to my heart. However, destiny had different ideas and I joined the voluntary staff of the global headquarters of the same Indian ashram, this time in upstate New York. Not only was this the headquarters but it was also a retreat site and I had a unique experience of living and working in an ashram. A 24-hour, 365-day-a-year immersion in a spiritual school. In the yogic tradition, the 'fire of yoga' is often referred to; a constant process of purification of the ego. My experience was just that, a challenge for all of us at the ashram to live to the highest, to have our spiritual goal as our guiding light. After three and a half years of imbibing the discipline of spiritual life I knew it was time to leave and take all my learning back out into the world.

In June 2001, my new partner and I moved to Southern Spain. It was there I completed my training to become a life coach and have run my practise ever since. Many of the stories and experiences in this book are informed not only from my own life journey but also others I have worked with.

We each have an individual journey, often being led to places we could not have imagined. Not only is this an adventure but it also has its ups and downs. Contemplating my life, I've come to realise that whereas in the past I thought I weathered storms and waited things out until they'd past, in fact life is actually comparable to a hurricane. Before I left the corporate world there were times when I thought that there was no storm, no hurricane. This was because I had unconsciously stepped into the eye, the calm centre. There were no unmet expectations, nothing to feel aversion towards; all was well with my world.

Nowadays, through what I've learnt in the past fifteen years, I know that I can reach that calm centre consciously. If I can keep myself in that centre then whatever is happening on the outside, a peace and contentment permeates my life. Now, don't go thinking that I live there always – far from it. I often whirl around in the outer edge of the hurricane, totally at its mercy and without any thought that this is an illusion at all. It feels real, scary, and at times, life-threatening. And then, just when I am totally caught up in the drama, something will get through to me and I will start the journey back to the centre.

That awareness is now available to me because of the commitment to apply my spiritual understanding to my life. It helps me at times of challenge; I have a far steadier mental and emotional state due to my focus. By changing my emphasis to being 'a spiritual being having a human experience' rather than 'a human being having a spiritual experience' it enables me to live 'centered'.

It takes self-effort to be this spiritual being, but on those days I'm Remembering Perfection.

Introduction

*It's not where you are going but rather
how you get there.
Remembering Perfection is the journey.*

There are days when I am seriously pissed off with God. I know I should know better, and some part of me does, but sometimes I want to join the majority of the world and blame someone. So, why not blame God? Lots of people do and it has to be someone's fault – I simply couldn't be in this mess on my own. But actually it is not God's fault at all. This book will show you how to take responsibility for your life so you'll no longer need to blame God or anyone else for that matter.

I know intellectually that it's not God's fault. The problem is that I often don't remember it. Especially the God 'out there' who I'm blaming in the moment. Why? Because as much as I know it is not God's fault, I also know there is not a God separate from me. I know this life is not as it seems on the outside. We are not separate from each other. At a deeper level we are all connected. We are all one in God. We are the Perfection. If you don't like the word God then it is totally interchangeable with The Universe, Source, Higher Self, Perfection, The Divine, Providence, or whatever term with which you feel most comfortable. At the end of the day it doesn't really matter what you call the energy that is us. This is not about the stereotypical image of God, it is about our deepest level of connection, the 'who' in 'who am I?' I believe we are all a spark of divinity, just as much as a drop of rain is part of the ocean. Therefore there is not a God separate from us with whom we can be annoyed. If I feel annoyed with God then I am actually annoyed with myself.

But that doesn't solve the living of it, does it? All the so-called negative emotions we feel are part of the living of it – part of living life spiritually. Applying all that I know in my life. Knowing it is one thing, experiencing it is another. I've read the books, agreed with the theory, listened to the talks, sat at the feet of a enlightened master and imbibed her words, but unless I live this, breathe this, make it part of my very being, it is worthless. A total waste of time.

If it's not where you are going but how you get there, how you live spiritually, then Remembering Perfection is the journey. This book explores the 'how' of living spiritually, the practical application of the spiritual principles that we probably have heard many times. Unconditional love, practising gratitude, being present, surrender – to name a few. It is designed to help you the reader move them from intellectual exercises into the realm of everyday living. It is time to move off the fence of 'wouldn't it be nice if we all lived like this' to 'from today I am going to live like this and be a light in the world'.

What does that mean, 'be a light in the world'? I believe that each and everyone one of us can influence the way our world is. From our individual interactions with those close to us, to people we meet for the first time, to people we never have or will ever meet. The attitude we bring to each and every interaction carries an energy that influences humanity as a whole. All great movements in our history have come from individuals standing up and making change. The one that comes to mind is the fall of the Berlin wall. When a large enough number of people stood up and said 'No' was when the change in Germany started to happen. That was an example of how people can change the world. Never think that you cannot make a difference, only you can make a difference in your world. As Mahatma Ghandi said as he led India to freedom, "You must be the change you wish to see in the world."

I follow a spiritual path. It is rooted in the scriptures of Kashmir Shavism, an ancient text written over 5000 years ago from Kashmir in India. One of its core teachings is 'God dwells within you as you'. It also teaches that God is everything in this universe, there is nothing that is not God. This whole universe is a manifestation of God. It is God experiencing God. Life is not one of separateness, of duality; rather we are all one being. Our life journeys are the path back to a complete experience of this, back to Perfection. This is the 'where' we are all going. We are here to learn the life lessons, to remove the veils from our eyes and see that we are divine in our essence. This has been a process over many lifetimes. As we purify the mind, the ego, we begin to see that all the things we get caught up in, all the things that make us feel separate are what stop us experiencing the truth of our divinity. As one great master said, "It is not that you have to attain anything, you already have it, you just have to remember it."

This book is not suggesting a specific way of understanding God but rather that you suspend the 'No' and replace it with 'Oh'. In other words, allow yourself to experience your world from a different perspective for a while. While you may not intellectually 'get' some of the ideas in this in book, allow yourself to at least feel them. Our understanding happens on many different levels and as you continue reading you will find that your experience will expand. Allow the book to unfold along with you. The great thing about exploring these worlds is that in one way or another it will help you find your truth. Something will resonate with you or not, either way it is your truth. There is never an only way – just another way. In my experience truth comes from the source, truth comes from God, from the heart. Truth always loves, always supports and always has our highest as its focus.

Most spiritual paths suggest practices – things to help us stay centred and aware of how things really are, aware of the Self, the true essence of who we are. You can use the word Self but you could replace it with many synonyms, Soul, Atman, Spirit, Higher Self, Pure Consciousness, the Witness. It is the part of us that is unchanging. When you are centred and aware it helps you see when you are in your heart and when the ego is running the show. When you are in your heart you are coming from love. When the ego is running the show you are not connected with your heart and often coming from a space of fear. The practises that help include practising gratitude, meditation, chanting and contemplation and study of spiritual texts.

Within this study of spiritual texts I also include many contemporary teachers who write about spiritual principles and have a lot to offer those on the modern spiritual path. *Remembering Perfection* is not about saying all those truths again; they all say it very well. It doesn't matter what path you follow or what beliefs you hold, the principles contained within this book can apply in your life. *Remembering Perfection* is about living your higher truths; the constant day-to-day remembrance and application of them.

Many days this can be a challenge. You may want to be cross with people, don't feel loving, and you can't see the divine in all, especially him or her. On those days you really cannot get the idea that everything happens for the best. But if every day you have the intention to bring these truths into your life, you can catch yourself being caught up in the illusion and make the conscious decision to step out of it. And, just in case you're thinking I've totally made it – I haven't, but I am working on it – as you can too.

This book is about the journey towards making it, the how you get to live in that centre. It is about putting theory into practise, how we learn from the triumphs and the disasters. In it I will relate personal stories, mine and others, that will illustrate some of the points. I have included exercises that will help you become more aware of your own tendencies and give you tips to put into practise when you see that you need to address a particular issue or tendency in your life. Each chapter also suggests a contemplation. This is a way of mining your own wisdom and gaining a greater understanding of how a practise can work in your life. You can use this book in many ways. Take a complete read through and mark the bits that resonate with you. Dip into specific chapters when a situation occurs in your life. When you find yourself saying, 'how could I have done that again?' take a look and see if the answer is held within the experiences shared here. We all learn from each other and I trust that you will resonate with some of this and that you too may learn to come back to awareness more quickly, more often and with a lighter heart.

Our lives are a work in progress. We are all moving towards being able to live fully in the world. We are addressing our old belief patterns, our conditioning from lifetimes past, our blocks that hold us back from creating an extraordinary life in an ordinary way. In this way we are all moving towards a time when we can live here, in this world right now, with full compassion and nothing needing to change.

When we truly know (not intellectually but spiritually) that God dwells within us and every living and insentient being, we will spiritually experience that everything happens for the best. When we can see this single lifetime as a single day in our many lifetimes, the perspective it brings shines a new light on the present experience. We will then be living in that space of non-duality. We will not suffer the world but rejoice in the wonder of its creation and know no separation from it. It starts with us. We will see through our worldly experience and have the inner knowing that each life is valid as it is in this dimension of lessons. That is the goal and the path to the goal. To find perfection in all things. There are some beautiful Sanskrit mantras that describe this perfectly

> Om pūrṇamadah pūrṇamidaṁ
>   pūrṇāt pūrṇamudacyate
> Pūrṇasya pūrṇamādāya
>   pūrṇamevāvaśiṣyate.
>
>   Om śāntih śāntih śāntih.

Om. That is perfect.
    This is perfect.
From the perfect springs the perfect.
    If the perfect is taken from the perfect,
the perfect remains.

    Om. Peace! Peace! Peace!

All the things we do to live a spiritual life are a remembrance. We start to re-member, put back together our wholeness, re-member it. We re-member that we are God. We re-member Perfection. We re-member that God dwells in everything. We re-member that we are not the body but the Soul. We re-member that it is not what we do but who we are. The list is endless. We have to remember all these things because we forget them as children. For a myriad of reasons we forgot that we are God.

I heard a beautiful story recently of a four-year-old girl who kept pestering her parents to be alone with her new baby sister.

They were hesitant as she would not say why, but in the end, as she was so insistent, they decided to allow her to be with the baby. They listened through a baby listening device, wondering what she was going to say. As they sat in the kitchen listening to the two children in the bedroom they heard the four-year-old say to the baby, "Tell me how it is with God, how does it feel? I'm forgetting already."

One of the gifts we can give our future, our children, our world, is to help our children remember, so that they do not have to go through such a long process of re-membering as we have to. We can live our lives as an example to the children, whether they be ours or someone else's, for if they see us in the space of remembrance they too will be more likely to stay there. Our children are our future, wouldn't it be a wonderful world if all people everywhere lived with the consciousness of God as everything; if we all Remembered Perfection.

So, where to start?

CHAPTER ONE

Gratitude

Gratitude is inviting God in.

Have you ever noticed that when things go well you don't blame anyone? I've just had a great few days. I have watched myself get into a flow. Life has not seemed as though I was pushing the river uphill. Things I've needed have come to me from unexpected directions allowing me to move forward with ease and joy. Today, as I sat down to my breakfast, looking out over the sea, I realised that because I had been feeling so good I had not been inspired to write anything for the last few days. It was almost as though no bad news equals nothing to write. Not annoyed with God – nothing to report. How one-sided is that?

A few years ago I was living in the ashram in upstate New York. It is a beautiful retreat site that many people visit throughout the year. Set in peace-inducing grounds, the ashram was offering a variety of courses and programs. People would come and study the spiritual teachings and also reconnect with themselves thus receiving new insights into life and its purpose. Sometimes impromptu discussions would take place in informal settings and one day we came together in the large upper lobby as one of the Swamis started to lead a discussion. She asked us to share with great honesty and simplicity something real about our lives. How what we had learnt in the time we spent at the ashram had helped us in our understanding. Everyone who stood up and talked about his or her lives shared something challenging, hard, difficult or negative. Not one person stood up and simply talked about how happy they felt about what they had in their lives. No one expressed how grateful they felt to have the opportunity to be on retreat and take time out. It was all focused on the negative situations, the challenges they felt that life dealt them.

There were probably 150 people in the room and after ten or so people had told their stories she stopped the discussion. She asked us to think why we thought to share something 'real' meant that it had to be about hardship – why couldn't we share something real about the successes in life. The fun times. Where was the gratitude in our lives? It was a very good question and one worth contemplating. As the discussion continued we began to see that it was simply a bad habit. People said that they felt uncomfortable talking about their triumphs; the common refrain was 'don't blow your own trumpet'. How often does this stop us talking about the good stuff?

Are you one of those people who talks about the bad stuff but feels that they can't share the triumphs? Does it feel like bragging or being superior? If so, take some time to ask yourself why. Are you one of those people who were told as children, "don't blow your own trumpet?" Do you feel self-conscious talking about something that you did well, that you shone in? The truth about being real is that you have to talk about the good and the bad, the negative and the positive. You have to show people a balance in life.

If you're going to tell people about what's not been going well also tell them about how you worked with it and turned it around. What is it that helped you get past the challenge? How did you get back into the flow of life? We can all learn from each other's life experiences. The more honest we are about them the greater the benefit not only to the listener but also for you. Another benefit is that whilst we talk about what we've learnt we can also gain more clarity about the situation. In her book, *Time to Think,* Nancy Kline talks about creating a learning environment. What she demonstrates is that as we talk about something we are also creating options, the simple act of talking and being heard allows the mind space to understand more and find solutions. Another benefit of talking openly and honestly is that we get to a place of gratitude for what we are learning.

And this brings me back to what I started to say – I haven't felt annoyed with God recently and so had not written anything. It was as if I only had something to say if it was negative. Where is the balance in that? I contemplated this and realised that what was missing was gratitude. Big word gratitude. Big truth. So what is gratitude? Why is it important? To me, gratitude is a completion of the energetic cycle of creation. It is the acknowledgment that there is something greater that we are all a part of and that we can recognise has an integral part in our lives. By thanking ourselves as well as God, we acknowledge that we are not separate nor are we alone in this life journey. We invite the energy of Grace, the divine supportive energy, into our lives through gratitude and are supported in all things. With that said how does gratitude manifest in our lives?

Gratitude in Friendship

This is one of many ways to be grateful. Not only is it part of friendship but it is also a way of being respectful. So often we tell our friends 'it's nothing' when they express their gratitude to us. We are effectively saying that it isn't necessary for them to voice their thanks. Not acknowledging their gratitude negates not only them, but also your contribution to their lives. Similarly, not voicing gratitude devalues the esteem you hold for someone. This can be the first step to taking or being taken for granted. I remember a conversation I had early on in my current relationship. We were talking about remembering to always say thank you for the everyday things we did for each other. Thank you for taking out the rubbish, for doing the washing, for making the bed. At first I found this odd, in my past relationships I had never acknowledged the everyday things. However, after a short time I began to see how important that basic gratitude was. It showed in a very simple and loving way that we did constantly acknowledge each other's contribution. Not only that but by learning the positive habit of noting these little tasks, we became more aware of each other and didn't feel like we were taking or being taken for granted. With this in mind, allow yourself to give and also accept gratitude and observe the respect it conveys. This is true friendship.

There are many situations in which we can be grateful. I am very grateful to my friend who offered a huge helping hand so that my life could flow again. It was at a time when I wanted to take a particular training course but it was beyond my reach financially and geographically. Out of the blue he offered an alternative solution that enabled me to move forward in my work without having to wait until I had saved the money. It also released me from feeling a victim in my financial circumstances. So, to him I am very grateful.

I am also grateful to another friend who reminded me that in order to move out of a stuck phase a few years ago I needed to reconnect with my practises. I needed to meditate, to contemplate certain circumstances, to go within to find my answers. I started to do this and from the outside it didn't seem like anything in particular was happening. However, inside me a peace began to settle, fears subsided and I noticed that in fact everything was all right. I began to see that it was my mind that was creating a lot of this havoc. I was so caught up in the fear of not being able to move forward that the fear itself was playing disaster scenarios. When I sat down quietly and thought about it I realised that it actually had no basis in truth. I could relax and move on. So I am very grateful to her for reminding me.

Is that it? No.

We can also be our own friend by being grateful to ourselves. I am very grateful to myself for hearing the forceful reminder and acting on it. We often miss that one – we often forget to thank ourselves for the self-effort we put in. It doesn't matter in what form Grace may come our way – we do need to put in the self-effort. The Grace of the divine and our own self-effort are like two wings of a bird, only with both can the bird fly.

We are taught at an early age to 'be grateful'. The learning by rote to say 'please' and 'thank you' as children. However, it is not this automatic 'thank you' I am talking about. It is the heartfelt gratitude that carries power. The one where we stop, even if only for a second, and drop into our heart and connect with love before giving gratitude. Gratitude is not the words, it is an energy that touches others and God.

So often in our busy lives we act from unconscious habit. We do things without actually connecting to them, like saying 'hello' to someone as we pass them in the corridor without even really seeing them. How often is our gratitude like this too? How do you give gratitude? Do you mean it as you are saying 'thank you' or is it a habit, words that simply come out of your mouth with no conscious thought? Next time you have the opportunity, choose to be truly grateful. Your recipient will feel the difference even if it is only shown with a smile. The energy behind true gratitude touches people deeply.

Gratitude as a Practise

Gratitude is a practise in itself. When things are off the wall we often pray for help. Sometimes the prayer is heartfelt, sometimes with anger and frustration – for God's sake help me! How often do we forget the gratitude? Not only the 'thank you' when things move and change but also gratitude as part of the prayer.

In most spiritual paths it is accepted that our minds co-create our reality. What we think is what we create and we will explore this in greater depth later. Gratitude can also be used in creating your reality. Affirmations, positive statements that can be part of the process of overcoming a negative belief, are always worded in the present tense, 'I am a successful speaker', for example. However, when gratitude is added it is a powerful boost to an affirmation. Not only can you word them in the present tense but also you can add gratitude to the mix. 'Thank you for inspiring me to be a successful speaker'. Gratitude pre-supposes the truth of the statement.

With a statement like that I can literally hear you saying, "but that's leaving everything to God, attributing everything to God, where am I in the process?" Where indeed? You are a pivotal piece of the process. True creation is a co-creation, this includes your self- effort. This gratitude does not mean that you do not participate. It means that you acknowledge that you have help – the divine help that is available to everyone. God can only help if you invite her in, not once but every time, all the time. Gratitude is inviting God in. And, when we invite God into our lives we live our truth. The ego is not a great one for gratitude. Sometimes we might pray for help and then think we've sorted it out ourselves. There is a great story about Sheik Nasrudin – he comes from the Indian tradition of using a person to humorously illustrate our human tendencies. Sheik Nasrudin had lost four gold coins and he was beside himself. He searched and searched for them and could not find them anywhere. Finally, he sat down, closed his eyes and prayed to God, "Please God help me find my gold coins and if I do I will give you half". He opened one eye to peek and there they were right in front of him. Immediately he cried out, "Not to worry, God, I've found them myself!"

Practising gratitude daily brings the awareness of gratitude into the forefront of your life. What is the purpose of this? Why do it? I asked a friend this question and her response was great. She said, "Because it's fun. It's acknowledging the blessings in my life, acknowledging what is. It changes the focus of my day and makes it lighter." What a great way to look at the world.

At least some time in the day remember to be grateful, leave yourself a reminder if you need to. I like to lie in bed at night before I go to sleep and say a prayer of gratitude. I once had a friend who used to set the alarm on her watch a couple of times a day to remind her – it drove us all up the wall but worked for her! Bring it into your day – how can you make gratitude a conscious action?

Sometimes it is useful to set an alarm to remind you to be grateful – whatever you're doing!

Be Grateful for Everything – the Good and the Bad

When you are practising gratitude don't judge whether something is good or bad. Simply practise gratitude. This might sound difficult but ask yourself this. Has there ever been a time when you have had something challenging and painful happen and you felt as though your world was falling apart? However, with hindsight you realised that it was the best thing that could have happened?

A client once told me of a sad break-up of her marriage, but as we talked and she reflected on what had happened she saw that it really was for the best. She realised that it had made her take a look at her life and start the process of standing on her own two feet. Because of this she began to do something with her life that she loved. She came to see that in fact she was very grateful for everything that had happened. By finding the gratitude she no longer regretted the marriage but could see it was part of her personal growth. In the same way she didn't regret the break-up. It was the next step.

Illness can also be a great teacher but again we have to step back to see the bigger picture. In her books, Caroline Myss, the medical intuitive, often talks about how our attitude to illness can be instrumental in the outcome. We often judge illness to be bad, but there are many people who have faced illness and saw that it was one of the most important teachers they had in their lives. Many inspirational books have been written by people with chronic or terminal illnesses who have completely turned their lives around both in the search for a cure and also because the illness came as a wakeup call. However, sometimes the lesson is that there may be no cure and it is for us to adjust to living with dis-ease and allowing it to be our teacher.

A lovely friend of mine was diagnosed with cancer and her journey through the seven years she had with the disease was one of great beauty. Towards the end of her life she talked about how her life had changed since she had been diagnosed. From being in the corporate sector, driven in her work with no time for herself, or those around her, she came to see that her life was not about her position in the corporate world. On changing her lifestyle she discovered a creative side to herself that had been hidden before. As she nurtured her creativity her time became one of self-healing and self-acceptance. A few weeks before she died she said that she had come to a place of total acceptance and that she was glad for her life – all of it. It had become so rich with love, she wouldn't have changed it. What an incredible place of gratitude.

For other people illness can be the wakeup call that will move them forward towards living life with greater awareness. It might be what makes them live healthier, eat better, take up exercise, give up smoking, cut back on the alcohol. It could take them out of a job that they actually hate but aren't brave enough to leave and push them in another direction in life. It may bring them into contact with a completely new set of people and open doors and bring opportunities that they could never have imagined. Even if illness does bring these benefits it can be difficult not to feel the victim of illness. Often the first reaction is one of 'why me?' As illness is playing out its magical alchemy we may feel that it is 'happening' to us, out of our control and we still might fight the changes. In these circumstances it is difficult to remember to be grateful.

When I talk about these types of situations with clients I am often told, sometimes angrily, that it is easy to be grateful with hindsight. I agree, it is. The challenge is to be grateful without the hindsight. It is very powerful to practise gratitude in the moment. If we can learn to be grateful, to practise it, we can then call on that strength when we need it most. During those times of crisis. Only by trying do we learn the benefits of gratitude and if truth be known, what have we got to lose?

I have had experiences when I've felt really let down by life. Those moments when yet another thing happens and it is the straw that breaks the camel's back. Often these are not huge challenges but more a culmination of things like the car breaking down just after I needed to pay out for a new printer. I felt a victim of life, of circumstance, of things outside my control. However, because gratitude is high on my list of things I do, I now often remember to practise gratitude in these moments. Because of my past experiences I know that if I can turn my attitude around then I can experience the world differently.

It is difficult to start off saying, for example, 'thank you for the car breaking down'. At this point your mind and your ego will be screaming, 'are you crazy, what are you thankful for that for?' It's not that it is great that the car broke down; you'll probably never know quite why that happened. But practising gratitude in the moment of upset, when you think things are going wrong will change your attitude to the situation and you will be able to handle it that much better. Moaning is a habit. We all do it but often if we stopped and really reviewed the situation we would see that actually everything is fine. We just like to whinge. I live in the beautiful sunny south of Spain. Many people move here because of the climate and the lifestyle it affords. But you would be amazed at how many people then spend the whole summer moaning about how hot it is. It is a human condition to find fault. Learning to practise gratitude creates a new way of being, seeing the good comes easier.

So in these moments when you choose to practise gratitude, start with where you are. Even if you do not feel grateful as you say, 'thank you for the car breaking down' keep on being grateful. Repeat to your self, 'Thank you for…' and just say whatever comes to your mind. You may start off with negative things but as you carry on you will start to think of the good things.

Things like, thank you for my health and that of my loved ones. Thank you for the food on my table and the music in my life. Thank you for the beauty of the local park, for the sunshine and the rain. Thank you for this wonderful gift of life, and for the home I have. Thank you for a child's giggle that brings laughter bubbling up inside of me. Thank you for the lessons I learn along the way – the list is endless. There is so much to be thankful for in this world – you need to widen the parameters. I have had days that have been turned around by this. I have felt low and ended feeling a wondrous joy at how blessed I am to have this life. Try it next time you feel let down by life, when you are having a good old moan. In fact I encourage you to make gratitude a regular exercise whether you feel lousy or great. How about right now?

Gratitude for the Lessons in Life

Our lives are a flow of continuous lessons whether we notice them or not. I once heard our human existence referred to as Earth School and it really resonated with me. As we move through the journey of life we are constantly learning lessons and being given gifts along the way. It is through this journey that we Remember Perfection.

If we practise gratitude for all the things in our life we will be going a long way towards living truth. Can you be grateful for lessons in your life whether they feel good or bad? Can you treat both these events equally? Can you step back and see the good in the bad? And be grateful?

By being grateful for our life lessons we learn to move through them with greater ease. We don't fight or resist them but become more open to what life is showing us right now. It becomes more natural to ask ourselves, 'What is this situation showing me about myself?' 'What pattern is being illustrated to me?' The old saying, 'what we resist, persists' is true and gratitude in these situations dis-empowers the resistance.

A friend of mine was having a hard time recently. He was feeling that everything, in his job and his relationship, was going haywire. He was coming to the end of his tether one day, not knowing what his next step was and feeling incredibly frustrated at the lack of movement on any front. We went out for a coffee and sat in the sun, always good for relaxation, and talked about what was happening. As he began to see the patterns in his life it became obvious that it was nothing to do with what was happening at that moment. Rather it had to do with his absolute need for control. Once he could see it I then suggested that he could start by being grateful for the lesson, for the insight. In this way he could start to let go and step back from the situation. By practising gratitude it loosened his grip on the need for a particular outcome. He stopped trying to manipulate the situation and the issues that had created the lesson in the first place started to be resolved.

It takes courage to be grateful for everything but it is worth it.

Always look for the gift in any situation.

IT MUST BE HERE SOMEWHERE...

Start by making this intention. The next time you're caught up in how awful something is, remember to look for the good in the situation, the lesson, the gift. Intention is a very powerful tool; you can use it in any situation. If you set an intention to remember to practise gratitude it can work like a subconscious computer program. Your intention will send a message onto your conscious screen, like those alert messages on the computer, and remind you. When this happens, remember to thank your mind for the message and it will remind you even quicker next time.

Gratitude and Grace

It is my experience that gratitude and Grace go hand in hand. A wonderful definition of Grace is that Grace is energy infused with prayer. I also think that it is infused with gratitude too. Grace, that invisible, divine energy that is available to us all, should we invite it in, is always present when we practise gratitude. Grace is the benevolent energy that supports us constantly, a source of love, a universal field that is present for us all, whatever the tradition we may follow. Grace is the divine energy of God and gratitude invites God in. By inviting God in through gratitude you are opening yourself up to a support beyond your imagination. Those co-incidences that surprise us so are another form of Grace. The everyday miracles that occur, and the big ones, the times we feel saved by Providence, the times that we feel in the flow of life, those moments when we just know that everything is as it should be are all infused with Grace.

So remember, on the days you're not annoyed with God, and the days you are, practise gratitude, invite God in. Remember Perfection, what have you got to lose?

Tips

- True gratitude is heartfelt; make it real every time. If you catch yourself offering lip-service gratitude, stop, breathe into your heart and connect with yourself and then offer the gratitude from that place.

- Acknowledge and voice gratitude to your friends, family and to your partner, especially for the everyday stuff – don't take things or people for granted.

- Remember to be grateful to yourself and your Self. You are doing ok!

- Set the intention to be grateful for whatever happens. Envision yourself dealing with a 'bad' situation with gratitude as well as a fun one too. This quote from Rudyard Kipling may remind you:

    > '...If you can meet with triumph and disaster
    > And treat those two impostors just the same...'

    Be grateful for both, this is true gratitude

- If you use affirmations, add the power of gratitude to the mix.

- Acknowledge your life lessons with gratitude. See them for what they gave you and by doing so you can begin to feel the gratitude for them.

- Make gratitude a daily practise; decide how and when you will do it. Is it five minutes before you go to sleep? Or perhaps you keep a gratitude journal where you list everything you are grateful for? Or can you set aside some time with your partner to share with each other what you are grateful for today? Choose one that you feel would work for you and commit to doing it. After a few weeks take stock, what has changed in your daily life because of practising gratitude?

Let gratitude infuse the Grace in your life – invite God in through gratitude.

Contemplation

Give yourself at least half an hour for this contemplation. If you have a place within your home where you meditate use this space or if not, just find somewhere quiet where you will not be disturbed. Have your journal or a notebook handy.

Before you start this contemplation identify one idea or phrase that stood out for you in this chapter. For example it might be the idea of gratitude being a practise. You now need to devise a question for you to contemplate. For example, it could be, 'what does it mean to practise gratitude?' Or 'how would practising gratitude manifest in my life?' Settle on whatever question feels right for you, something that will give you insight into the idea.

Get into a comfortable position and gently relax your body by taking some deep breaths. Breathe into any area of your body that holds tension and as you breathe out feel the tension flowing out with your breath. Once you feel relaxed bring your breathing back to your normal rhythm and simply focus on your breath for a few minutes. At this point invite Grace into your contemplation in whatever way seems appropriate for you. Now ask yourself the question you wish to contemplate. Ask it three times and then simply sit and see what comes to mind. If you find your mind wandering simply bring it back to the question. After sitting with the question for a while pick up your pen and begin to write. Let the answer flow, do not censor it, stop it or word-craft it. Simply allow your wisdom to emerge. Once you have finished sit quietly for a moment and acknowledge the wisdom and insight received.

CHAPTER TWO

See God in Each Other

*See God in Each Other
— the ultimate level of respect.*

See God in each other. That is a big statement and one that sometimes stops people's minds. It did mine when I first heard it. It can also be said in different ways: we are all one, God dwells within you as you, we are not separate from God. You may have also heard other versions. However much my mind agrees with this – and it does whole-heartedly – it is not always my reality, not my always experience. This is a key point when we talk about anything spiritual, especially applying spiritual truths. We can understand something intellectually; our mind grasps a fact and agrees with it. It is a different thing entirely to experience it. Until we experience something it is simply in the realm of the intellect.

For example, I can be told what Cornish vanilla ice cream tastes like, – kind of creamy, sweet, cool and caramelly, but until I actually eat it myself I cannot experience it. Then my experience will be personal to me. I will sense the texture, the sensation of eating something cold, the taste of vanilla and that idea of thick Cornish cream. Only from that experience can I know what eating Cornish vanilla ice cream is like. The same applies in our spiritual life. Until we experience it for ourselves it is an abstract idea, having no substance and definitely no taste.

When I first heard the principle 'see God in each other' I didn't know exactly what it meant. I had no experience of it, no reference point. I had heard the idea that God is not someone/thing separate from us. The idea that we each hold a spark of divinity rang true if not a little impersonal. Other than my experience in the personal development course which had launched my spiritual search, my 'You are God' moment, it was not something I was regularly aware of. As I learnt, though, it is possible to glimpse the divinity in all things in many ways. As we will explore in this chapter, nature, music and meditation are some of the different ways that people experience God. These experiences are the doorway to understanding the principle of seeing God in each other. Once we identify these moments we can then take it to the next level and expand the principle, and our experience, to specifically seeing God in each other.

I remember the first time I 'got' the idea of everything being God. The sudden 'aha' moment. I was taking a walk with a friend in Savernake Forest in England. It is a very old forest, with beautiful beech trees that leave a thick carpet of red and rustic leaves in autumn. As we rustled our way through the leaves we were talking about the principle of God in everything. We stood admiring a huge ancient beech tree, low branches beckoning to be climbed, its solid roots spreading out into the chalky soil, and my friend said that it wasn't that God was *in* the tree, separate from the tree, but that God *was* the tree. There was nothing about the tree that was not God. At that moment it felt as though I had 'remembered' a truth.

Nature can often hold these moments of truth. Many spiritual teachers will suggest that you take time out to be in nature, to be inspired by nature, to be woken up by nature. It has regularly been my experience. If you feel the need for a change in perspective, often nature will provide the setting.

When I was living in upstate New York I used to have a particular walk in the mountains that would bring me clarity and insight. I didn't have a car at that time but a friend always used to know when I needed to take that walk – she'd come up to me and hand me the keys to her car and I'd take myself off for the afternoon and go up to the mountains. This particular walk had magnificent views all the way to the horizon. It was in the middle of a huge forest, dissected by running, bubbling streams. My walk was atop a rocky outcrop, like an inland cliff. Being on top of the bluff I used to find that the change of outer perspective, seeing far into the distance, changed the inner perspective too. As my outer vision expanded so did my inner vision, I felt much more aware of the interconnectedness of the Universe. If you need to reconnect with the divinity of the world then nature can hold your key.

Nature isn't the only way we can experience the divine. I have a friend who gets totally lost in music, especially Bach. To her, the complexities of the composition literally blows her mind, in other words, thought stops as she surrenders to the music. To reconnect through music can be a divine experience. The Indian tradition speaks of a divine music that can be heard in meditation. It is called Nāda and can only be described as celestial blissful music. It is other-worldly and cannot be likened to anything we produce in a recording studio. Music unites the two hemispheres of the brain and induces a deep relaxation and creates the right conditions to experience the perfection of the moment. Sometimes, during a meditation or chant, time stands still and everything is perfect, complete, whole.

Have you ever had an experience of everything being perfect, that nothing had to change? It could have been in nature or listening to a piece of music, or being in a special place. Each person's experience is unique but may often hold a feeling of deep, ancient inner peace. It can also be a feeling of being connected to everything, nothing being separate from you. The day might be clearer, the air sparkling, a feeling of heightened sensitivity to everything and everyone around you. Or sometimes it can be a pure feeling that nothing in the world has to change right now, an inner and outer perfection. Cast your mind back, have you experienced anything similar? Take yourself back into that feeling, it is a clue to not only your divinity but also the divinity of the world around you.

Somehow the idea of God *as* everything feels different, easier to absorb than God as each other. God as each other feels too personal, almost arrogant. How do we get from understanding the theory, and maybe the experience of God as everything, to the practise of seeing God in each other?

Seeing God in each other is the ultimate form of respect. If we can master this view of the universe then our interactions will be filled with love and respect for the world and each person in it. Seeing God in each other is another way of practising unconditional love, something we will look at later. If our aim in life is to live in harmony with each other, applying what we know to be spiritual principles, then seeing God in each other is a pivotal part of that. When we truly live this we honour all things and in doing so our lives become more dynamic, more real and in the present. How do we do it? How to remember in each interaction that God dwells in every person? How do we remember that God is every person? Not only that, but also that God is everything – this whole universe is God.

Practising Seeing God in Each Other

One way is to pretend. Act as if – pretend – practise – fake it till you make it – create the reality! Whichever way you look at it, it has to be a conscious decision. The most difficult part of living applied spirituality is remembering to do it. By 'acting as if' we start to set up a conscious habit, a good habit. In the end it will become our mode of operation but until we have it off pat, without thought, we need to find a way to remember. 'Acting as if' is one way to create conscious action.

Seeing God in each other had not been a regular practise for me, but a few years ago I decided that I would put it to the test and start to cultivate a habit of seeing God in each other, treat everything/one as God. In my experiment I managed to remember at the beginning and the end of my working day – why? Because I have to deal with Spanish drivers! I remembered because they annoyed me. They annoyed me a lot. They drive so close you can see a pimple on their nose. They specialise in overtaking on blind corners, especially when there is traffic coming the other way. And, on top of it all, if you slow down to let someone through or stop to let someone out of a side road they do not even acknowledge you. Not a single sign of a thank you – nothing, zilch, nada. So, there I was, daily cursing all the Spanish drivers to hell and back when I realised that this would be a very good moment to start practising seeing God in everyone.

Practise with something that drives you up the wall.

YOU MUST BE ENLIGHTENED IF YOU CAN SEE GOD IN SPANISH DRIVERS!

Now this might sound an odd time to start such a practise – an act as if – but the more bizarre the starting place the easier it is to remember. After all, that is what we are doing here – remembering. This is nothing new; we know this, all of it, we simply have to remember. At first it felt false, like a lip service, but as I carried on it began to feel more real. I found my frustration levels dropped immensely, I could simply smile whereas before I would have been angry. Gradually, it began to percolate into other areas of my life and I find today that often, especially when I am annoyed, I remember to take that step back, pause and see God in each other. As time went on I came to see that there were other aspects to seeing God in each other. Different things that could help me achieve it. Compassion was one thing, giving blessings was another.

Compassion Helps

I used to get very confused when I first started learning the various spiritual truths. I used to think that if you see God in everyone you would therefore have to love everyone and welcome them into your life, whoever they were. It felt like it was saying 'become a door-mat'. I envisioned becoming the type of person that allows herself to be treated disrespectfully because she doesn't want to be nasty and say 'enough'.

Then my vision began to get slightly clearer in that you can see God in everyone but that doesn't mean you have to love the ego in everyone. You don't have to like all those strange personality quirks that are in each of us, the ones that are not a true reflection of the Self. There will always be people in our life that we have a reaction to, whether it be a family member, boss or a politician we simply do not agree with. So far, so good. However, I then remembered that to have aversion to anyone or anything is just a personal ego reaction. That ego reaction was also not the Self. We know that our goal is to see God in everyone. It is also to have aversion to no one, no thing. Where does that leave you when you can't stand someone and really do not want anything to do with them? How do you see God in them?

Compassion is one of the keys to this riddle. Compassion for the other person and compassion for yourself. You can have compassion for someone and in doing so drop judgement and accept them as they are. You can see the God within, but at the same time have compassion for yourself and choose not to be around them. As for aversion, we can also be compassionate with ourselves when we feel it. We are still on the journey, learning to apply these principles and sometimes our buttons get pushed and we don't like something or someone. And that's ok as long as we continue to practise and learn to see the God in each other whenever we remember. By focusing on the God within we see past the ego, the bit we have the reaction against, and recognise the Soul.

Send Blessings, Drop Judgement

With this in mind I can choose to see God in Spanish drivers but I don't have to choose to support their driving or emulate it. It is up to you which people, and what energy you surround yourself with. You can choose, without condemning anyone, whether you wish to be in the company of certain people. On one of her tapes, Caroline Myss said: "you confuse the hell out of me – bless you – I'm outta here!" I love this – the possibility to have compassion, bless someone (or thing) and choose not to be in their energy is such a freeing notion. To give blessings is to send a positive thought, energy and love towards another. By seeing God in each other we are giving blessings. And it works. You don't feel judgmental because you are accepting of who they are in this moment. You feel compassion not derision for where they are (be aware if you start to feel superior – that is not the aim) and you are giving love through blessings. It boils down to love; finding a way to be love in this world. In this way you are not annoyed with God – just blessing God and choosing to go find him or her in another form.

If in doubt send blessings.

So there I was sending blessings left right and centre to all Spanish drivers and you know something, it felt good. It felt good to be in that space of positivism, not to be superior and deride everyone for their lack of ability or gratitude. My drive to and from work felt easier, less stressful and I was able to see the beauty of the day, the good things in life. It was a small but subtle shift and it was one small step.

It can sometimes feel overwhelming, this idea of 'acting as if'. However, this is one way of applying spirituality to our everyday lives. How can we 'act as if', pretend to live in that space of the Self? Especially when we constantly forget and are at the mercy of our conditioned reactions. Well, here is a starting place. Give yourself a small task to accomplish each day. I didn't berate myself at the end of the day for forgetting to 'see God in everyone' I met. I had set myself the task of seeing God in Spanish drivers. Now this may sound little and, sure, anyone can do that – but can you? Can you set yourself the task of seeing God in a certain person or place? Can you send blessings instead of getting annoyed? Practise it – for when you've got it as a habit then you can expand it. Little steps move big mountains.

Forgiveness

Forgiveness is another element of seeing God in each other. When we are not able to forgive someone for something we are miles away from seeing the divinity of a situation, let alone a person. Forgiveness can be one of the hardest practises that we are asked to do on the spiritual path. It means we have to drop anger, blame, criticism, judgement, aversion, pride, expectations and many others emotions that we might be feeling. It does not, however, mean that we have to condone a situation or action. Forgiveness is the dropping of the negative feeling held within ourselves, the letting go of an emotion that in the end only harms us.

If you are feeling resentful and wish to get revenge what energy is coursing through your system? Think about it. Think about a situation in which you cannot forgive someone or something. A situation in which there is no way you can see God in that person. How does it feel in your body? What is going through your mind? Who is being destroyed in this process? Is it the person you are constantly sending your vital energy to in the form of resentment? Or is it you who is the loser? Are you the one who is leaking energy and therefore depleting yourself? Or even worse, are you eating yourself up inside for something you cannot forgive yourself for? How better would you feel if you could drop that self-destruction? If you would let go of that negative feeling?

I was talking with a client one day about forgiveness. She could not, would not, forgive her boss for treating her in such an off-hand manner. The company she worked for had to let people go as it was in financial difficulties. She felt she had not been treated well when she was told that she was one of those who were being made redundant. Listening to the story, I could see on one level that she had a legitimate complaint. However, it also sounded like the person who was her boss did not have the appropriate people skills and was probably embarrassed to have to do the job of telling people they were to be made redundant. This level of communication is an art and as with most situations there are two sides to any story. I suggested that her anger was actually in detriment to herself, her feeling of need for revenge only reflected back on her, and that maybe it would be good for her to forgive her boss so she could move on.

To forgive was not to condone what he did, but a way for her to stop focusing all her energy on something from the past. This forgiveness is a way of seeing God in each other. By letting go of past hurts we are moving past the personal, the physical, and seeing the best in someone, even if they don't see it or act like it themselves. This forgiveness acknowledges that we are all not perfect, but that when we look higher, above the reactions of our egos, we reach the responses of our Self. The God within me sees the God within you.

One understanding that helps in these kind of situations is that everyone is doing the best they can with the resources they have available to them. We all have every resource available to us but not everyone has access to these resources. For example, if someone is not acting in an understanding way it is because that resource is not part of them. If they could be understanding they would, for no-one wants to be less than they are. In the example above her boss could not have dealt with the situation any other way as he didn't know how. Forgiveness understands that each and every person is doing the best they can – we may think it is awful but it is still the best they can.

In her book, *Stranger in Paradise,* Julie Chimes talks about her experience of forgiveness of the woman who tried to stab her to death. A truly horrific story; from the outsider's point of view, it demonstrates the depth of forgiveness that some people are challenged with and shows the depth of the human spirit in forgiveness. To be able to tell her attacker that she loved her as she was being attacked is Remembering Perfection.

Once you have decided to forgive either yourself or someone else there are things you can do on different energetic levels. Not all of these may appeal or be possible, but they are all tools for forgiveness. You can take some time to be honest with yourself about what happened. Get yourself into a quiet space and review the situation as it occurred. Looking at what happened, be honest about everyone's responsibility. It is never one-sided and, even though you may feel a victim of circumstance or a cause of upset, I can assure you that each party had a part to play. Once you have reviewed the occurrence and seen the parts played by each, ask yourself 'is there anything that needs to happen on a physical level so that I can forgive and move on.' Do you need to discuss what happened or make some reparation for something you said or did? If you feel that this is the road to forgiveness then start taking steps to do something. Be warned though, forgiveness does not need an action by another person, this is not 'I will forgive if you do xxx'. True forgiveness is getting to that place within yourself alone. To be in a position where you can honestly say you have forgiven. It is a feeling within the body, not a thought within the ego.

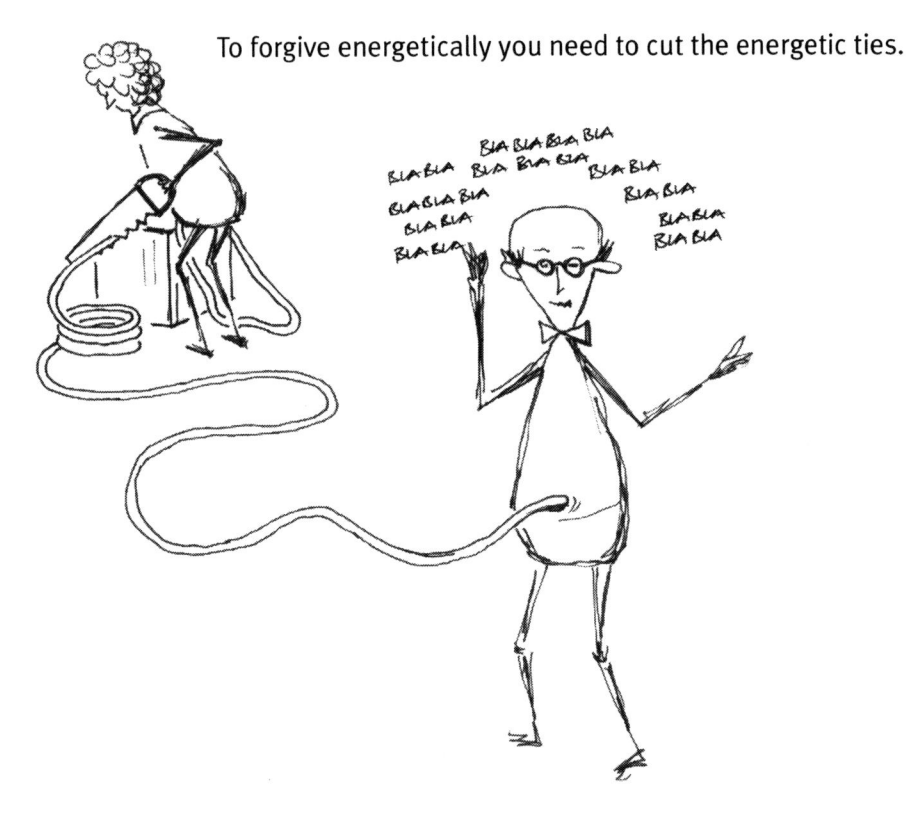

To forgive energetically you need to cut the energetic ties.

Another level of forgiveness is to forgive on an energetic level and withdraw your energy from it. Each day we feed old resentments through our energetic body without even being conscious of doing so. Your lack of forgiveness drains you of energy. A good exercise is to become aware of this. Find a quiet space and focus your attention on the old situation that you feel you have not yet forgiven. Feel in your body where your energy is flowing out to this old pain and consciously bring it back. You can do this by feeling or visualising this energy leaving your body. Once you are aware of it, see yourself bring this energy back into your own body. Feel it flow back to you and cut the ties with the old situation, envision the flow breaking and closing down the avenue, like a road-block. Once you become aware of how your energy leaves you to feed an old resentment you can daily bring it back at the same time as offering forgiveness. One day you will realise that it is done, you have forgiven and moved on. Forgiveness is a great healer and allows us to see God in each other once again.

Asking for Help

When you decide to practise seeing God in each other, choose something that bugs you. If you try this with something or someone that you really like it will not be as easy to remember. Reason being that when you love someone or thing you kind of see God in them anyway. That's why you love them. Choose someone or something that really gets under your skin and ask for the Grace to remember each time. By asking for help you will find that as soon as you start to berate something or someone in your mind, you will be reminded of compassion and blessing. Always remember to ask for the support of Grace – to ask for help. As I said earlier, you need to constantly invite God in to your life not just once but over and over again. Inviting Grace is inviting God. Pray, in whatever way you pray, for the help to remember, and know that no prayer goes unanswered.

I learnt this lesson a few years ago. I was having great trouble getting an old lover out of my mind. The constant yearning was getting to be very exhausting and all I could think of was why were we not together, what had I done wrong, why were we no longer in contact – on and on it went. One day I made the decision it was time to stop. However, I knew I needed help. So

I prayed. I prayed that whenever my mind went to this person, God would show up instead. My part of the deal was that when God showed up I would then contemplate God. By simply becoming present and focusing on the God within I could step back from all the thoughts that were crowding my brain. You know something – it worked – right from the outset it worked. Within a couple of weeks of this constant practise I stopped obsessing. I had let go of the attachment and I felt free. Life could move on. I felt grateful for the lesson, the change in my focus and the support I had had in making it happen.

Ever since then I realise that I can pray for this level of assistance. If I want to break a habit or change my subconscious way of thinking, judging or being then I need to make a firm intention, pray for help and fulfil my side of the deal when the help arrived. Now this is important too – I have caught myself when given this moment of choice, especially when dealing with anger – do I get annoyed or do I give love? Sometimes something in me doesn't want to be loving – it wants to be angry – it wants to be nasty. This is what I mean by keeping my side of the deal – I need to fulfil my promise to choose love. I can also pray for the strength of character to make that choice. Not always easy I grant you and I don't always make it, but all I have to do is recommit to it when I catch myself.

I invite you to think of something that you would like to change; a person or situation in which you wish you could truly see God and commit to doing so. Ask for the help in whichever way is your way and see what happens. See how the reminder comes. If you do this for long enough you will find that instead of thinking the negative, being reminded and then thinking the positive you will skip the first two bits and simply see God and send blessings.

I remember someone I met in the ashram who had decided to make this practise of seeing God in each other her main practise and contemplation for three years. She recalled how difficult it was for her as she had always been an overcritical person. Once she saw this trait in herself she decided that seeing God in everyone was the perfect antidote. She committed to starting each meeting with an internal prayer to see God in everyone. Gradually, as she became more aware, she expanded that commitment to all interactions in her life. It was not easy and she prayed for the resilience to carry on when her ego fought back with great force. But over time, through her commitment to change and honesty about how she was doing, change did occur. People started to tell her how much softer and loving she was, how much more approachable she had become at work. She realised people sought her and her opinion out instead of avoiding her and her razor-sharp tongue. She was so grateful to herself for her effort and for the support she felt she received from God. The constant reminders, challenges, successes and good feedback she got as she made a positive change in her life, fuelled by her self-effort, allowed her to become a greater version of herself. And it showed.

When we live in the Self, when we see God in each other, we are giving the ultimate form of respect. The practise of it reminds us of God in our lives. When we get caught up in the helter-skelter of life it helps us stop, take a breath and remember the divinity in life. It gives us the experience of appreciation for all those around us. This appreciation for life makes the day seem brighter; you see the beauty around you in whatever form it takes. Everyday interactions are more profound, real, and your heart sings. You are at peace.

And, you can Remember Perfection.

Tips

- If you want to reconnect with divinity try being in nature. Go out and discover a place where you can feel the energy of nature, uninterrupted by the busy world, a place where you can change perspective both outer and inner. Feel what happens in your body as you relax into the perfection of the moment. Remember that you can always take time to go there when you need to reconnect.

- To start a practise of seeing God in each other: Pretend – Act as if. As you do it more often you will set up a positive repetition until it becomes real for you. To do this, start seeing God in each other by giving yourself a small task to accomplish. Choose one situation or person to start with. Make it something that annoys you a lot or holds an energy for you – it will be easier to remember.

- To help you get into the feeling of seeing God in each other, take yourself back into a feeling of a time when all was perfect, when you felt a connection to everything, to the divinity in all. How does your heart feel? What was the physical sensation? If you don't have that experience ask yourself, how do I think it might feel? Let your imagination give you some ideas. Store this feeling within so you can access it when you wish to change your attitude to one of seeing God in each other. By bringing this sensation back into your awareness it will help you extend that connection to another.

- In your interactions in the world with the myriad of personalities you will encounter, have compassion and acceptance. Remember, you don't have to love the personality traits – just see the God within.

- Send blessings to as many people as you encounter – this brings you to a place of love and is another way of seeing God in each other.

- Forgiveness is a key to seeing God in each other. Check out those people and situations you still carry around unforgiven. Is it time to let go? If so, either do the exercises below or if you need to, work with someone to resolve these issues. Forgiveness is part of seeing God in each other.

- Remember, each person is doing the best they can with the resources they have available to them, no-one wants to be less than they are, therefore have compassion: forgive.

- To start to forgive, get yourself into a quiet space and review the situation as it occurred. Be totally honest about everyone's responsibility in what happened. Once you have reviewed the occurrence and seen the parts played by each person, ask yourself; 'is there anything that needs to happen on a physical level so that I can forgive and move on?' If you feel that this is the road to forgiveness then start taking steps to do something. Be warned though, forgiveness does not need an action by another person, this is not, 'I will forgive if you do xxx'. True forgiveness is getting to that place within yourself alone. It is a feeling within the body, not a thought within the ego.

- To start to let go energetically of past situations and forgive, find a quiet space and focus your attention on the situation. Feel in your body where your energy is flowing out to this old pain and consciously bring it back. You can do this by feeling or visualising this energy leaving your body. Once you are aware of it, see yourself bringing this energy back into your own body. Feel it flow back to you and cut the ties with the old situation, envision the flow breaking and closing down the avenue, like a road block. Once you become aware of how your energy leaves you to feed an old resentment you can daily bring it back at the same time as offering forgiveness.

- As with all our endeavours, ask for help, we are not unsupported in our journey, ask for help along the way. Be grateful for the form it comes in.

Contemplation

Give yourself at least half an hour for this contemplation. If you have a place within your home where you meditate use this space or if not just find somewhere quiet where you will not be disturbed. Have your journal or a notebook handy.

Before you start this contemplation, identify one idea or phrase that stood out for you in this chapter. For example, it might be the idea of being in touch with the God within as a way to learn to see God in each other. You now need to devise a question for you to contemplate. For example it could be 'how can I come to know the God within?' Or 'what can I do to remember to see God in each other?' Settle on whatever question feels right for you, something that will give you insight into the idea.

Get into a comfortable position and gently relax your body by taking some deep breaths. Breathe into any area of your body that holds tension and as you breathe out feel the tension flowing out with your breath. Once you feel relaxed bring your breathing back to your normal rhythm and simply focus on your breath for a few minutes. At this point invite Grace into your contemplation in whatever way seems appropriate for you. Now ask yourself the question you wish to contemplate. Ask it three times and then simply sit and see what comes to mind. If you find your mind wandering, simply bring it back to the question. After sitting with the question for a while pick up your pen and begin to write. Let the answer flow, do not censor it, stop it or word-craft it. Simply allow your wisdom to emerge. Once you have finished, sit quietly for a moment and acknowledge the wisdom and insight received.

CHAPTER THREE

Being Real

*Being real starts inside,
the highest form of self honesty.*

These two words, being real, invoke a feeling of honesty that our Souls crave. Our minds like the idea too. But what in our everyday life does it mean, being real? Firstly, we can be real with ourselves. Be aware of what story we are spinning to ourselves to justify an action or give ourselves an excuse for why we haven't done something. We can also be real in our dealings with each other by being in integrity. This can be through honesty, kindness, non-judgement, compassion, and love. Being real in business is another conundrum that we deal with daily. How to clinch that deal, get someone to do a task they don't want to do without manipulation, be honest when you know that this piece of information is the last thing someone wants to hear. How can you work in a way that honours who you are and the business you work in or for?

There is also the energetic level of realness, actually feeling sorry when you say so, or feeling compassionate when we act it. How often are our actions not congruent with our thoughts or energy? All these things have an element of being real and this is what we will explore, how we can still stay true to our essence when pulled in so many different directions in our lives. Why do we need to be real in our lives? Why make the effort to stay true to who we are? Simply, because our lives will be richer in every sense. Our relationships will be deeper, our working lives will hold a greater sense of purpose and we will feel more comfortable with ourselves, with our place in the world.

Being Real with Ourselves

In some ways this is the toughest area of being real. It is the area we can hide from the world. No one can know what we are telling ourselves and therefore it is tempting to side-step any awkward feelings, believe our story and avoid facing the truth. Being real with ourselves is to own every aspect of who we are and how we tick. It is taking responsibility for our emotions, reactions and responses. Often when we want to blame someone else (or God) for an event, it is because we are not able or do not want to be real with ourselves and own up to our part in the situation.

A client I was working with came face to face with this issue recently. He was taking a course to become a Sports Massage Therapist. The course had assignments to complete along with personal mentoring and practise sessions, but the timeline was completely under his control. As he got nearer to completing the course and going out there to get new clients – crunch time – suddenly many different and urgent things started to clamour for his attention. Not only that, but his practise clients started to re-schedule their appointments.

We set out to explore why this was happening and he came up with many legitimate reasons as to why he hadn't embarked on the last two assignments as well as the good reasons his clients had for cancelling. On face value they all sounded viable. However, he had taken the easier route of choosing to believe these reasons rather than dig deeper and face why he was avoiding completing the course. The fear of moving into the real world of creating a massage therapy practise, marketing his service and, crucially, finding out whether it was going to work or not, was spurring him on to procrastinate using as many different diversions as he could find. By his own admission if he had a choice of finishing his assignments or doing something else less taxing the 'something else' won – even if it was just the washing up!

As we looked deeper into his situation he began to see that his clients were mirroring his avoidance back to him. He wasn't committed to the massage therapy so neither were they. He kept re-scheduling and so did they. Often if we look at our personal circumstances we will see mirrored back to us what is going on in our own lives. This was a classic example. If you want an insight into your own situation, if you want to start being real to yourself, it is useful to ask yourself what is happening around you and then apply the answer to yourself.

Sometimes the mirror is an identical reflection as in this case and sometimes an opposite reflection, the shadow being revealed. For example, if we have drawn a lot of negative people or situations to us what fear or shadow are they showing us? Or is it maybe that we are being shown what we don't want in our lives? A tendency we have that we need to be aware of? Mirroring is a useful tool to be aware of, but you need to be honest and real with yourself to interpret them clearly. Ask yourself many questions from different angles until you reach the ah-ha answer, the one that hits the nail on the head.

Once my client became aware that he was stopping any chance of completing the assignments he could create the intention to change the pattern. He could also become vigilant as to when he was not being honest with himself, when he was not being real. Often, when this scenario is playing out in our lives it is totally unconscious. Of course there are times when we consciously decide to fool ourselves. One self-deception I have used a few times is that chocolate has no calories after 9.00pm when I've had a taxing day! However, more often than not this not-being-real is a habit that is so ingrained that we do not notice it. When I pointed out what was going on he could immediately own up to it, but until then he hadn't even seen it.

It is sometimes useful not only to ask ourselves what is happening around us, but also to talk with someone we trust who knows us well and see if they can shed any light. It can be an uncomfortable process as it can feel like we have been caught out. On some levels this is true, but is it not better to open our eyes to what we are doing rather than carry on using the same old excuses, however uncomfortable it is? If we have the intention to be as real as we can at all times, we will begin to notice when we are allowing ourselves to believe the excuse and then we can choose to change it.

Living the intention of being real can also bring changes into our lives, it challenges us to move on, grow, and honour our energy within a situation. This can feel uncomfortable as it takes us out of our comfort zone and at times we may resist it, but the benefits far outweigh the temporary feeling of discomfort. We each have our own comfort zone, the area in which we can operate without feeling stretched to experience or do new things. Surrounding that is our stretch zone, the place it feels uncomfortable and challenging to enter. This is where we learn to grow, try new things, take risks. Surrounding this stretch zone is the panic zone where we become frozen and cannot function. The rabbit in the headlights feeling. There is no point pushing ourselves into the panic zone but every

WOW!!! THIS IS GREAT! I CAN EVEN WEAR A SIZE 12!

Living in the stretch zone brings its own rewards.

reason for living in the stretch zone as much as possible. What happens when we live there? It becomes part of our comfort zone. As we expand as human beings, as we grow our comfort zone, we live our highest potential possible in the moment. This can be exhilarating, a feeling of freedom, a possibility to do anything and fulfil dreams. Being real brings us out of hiding and places us squarely in the centre from where we can shine.

Being Real with Others

Being real with others is a challenge for most of us at some time or other. Many of us think we are real when in fact it is just our ego playing out. For example, the rebel, the teenager with all the piercings and the attitude to match, thinks they are being real. But what is the motivation to be the rebel? Many people think the rebel is trying to show off; more often than not it is a huge mask to hide behind. Instead of revealing themselves, they show the world the mask, it feels safe when they cannot been 'seen'. Isn't that just another pattern, a way of hiding vulnerability? Being real can feel very unsafe, vulnerable, risky. Risking of being judged different. Risking of not conforming to society's expectations. Fear of ridicule, fear of failure, fear of letting people see the real us, of standing up and saying this is who I am. How often do we hide our vulnerability, play the game of being someone else in case the real us is not acceptable?

A client I was working with asked me how I thought she should react to something her new boyfriend had said. He had made fun of people who genuinely wanted to improve themselves and how they lived their lives. He couldn't see the point of changing a fun, fast-living lifestyle for a boring one of healthy living, moderation and self-enquiry through personal growth courses (his perspective). In truth, he probably felt threatened by such changes and in these circumstances attack is often the best form of defence. She was upset that this was his position and didn't agree with him but was unsure of what she should say in case he took offence. She wanted the 'right' answer, the safe answer that ensured the continuance of the relationship. What she didn't understand was the personal cost to her of such an answer. At that point I asked her, "why would you want to play at being someone you are not?" I pointed out that if this relationship were to continue then she would also have to constantly be someone she is not. I suggested that perhaps she should say what she thought and if he didn't like it then it was a pretty good indication that he wasn't the man for her. If he couldn't take a conflicting idea then why would she want to stay with him?

Amazingly this idea had never occurred to her. After talking it through she decided that she did want to be herself. It wasn't easy but she felt so empowered by standing up and stating who she was that in the end she decided that she didn't want to continue with the relationship. She could see that it didn't serve her and who she was and that the compromise to stay with him was too big. What she feared most – his leaving her – was actually what she chose in the end. The lessons she learnt in this situation gave her the confidence to be herself in the future.

So often we are so tied into what people might think, whether they like us or not, that we forget that we have to like ourselves first. Be ourselves first, be real. We learn to compromise who we are in order for the world to like us. If we can practise being real in moments like this then it makes it easier to practise being real in other situations too. By learning to be real and vulnerable in our relationships we can find it easier to take it into our everyday interactions with others in the world.

It is commonly thought that to be vulnerable is to be weak. One of the dictionary definitions of vulnerable is 'to be open to criticism'. This does not mean that we have to be injured by criticism. Rather, to be strong enough to hear it and deal with it. When we commit to being real with each other we need to cultivate a comfort with our vulnerability. This is the strongest position. If you can genuinely be vulnerable, be open, and not worry what people think or how they might judge you then you can stand strong, honour your own feelings and be real. From that position no-one or no-thing can harm you, you have nothing to fear. True vulnerability is strength.

Being real is often accompanied by a feeling of nervousness – the kind of feeling we get when we fear a particular outcome. This nervousness is a great sign, a sign that we are on the right road. I was talking with a friend, who is a public speaker, about the pitfalls of giving a presentation and how she used to feel nervous before an audience. Standing up in front of so many people, looking out at all those expectant faces, some friendly and smiling and some closed and judging. She used to feel nervous of being open and real in front of so many people as she knew that they were all going to have an opinion about what she said, who she was and how she spoke.

She changed this by realising that that nervousness was simply an energy. It could be interpreted in any way she wanted. She began to choose to interpret the energy as the energy of the universe, she called it the Shakti, a Sanskrit term for the universal divine energy of consciousness. When she felt this energy she knew that she was in touch with the God within and from that point she could go out there feeling totally supported in being real. And wow, was she some speaker! She spoke from the heart, you could feel her truth in what she said and each time I heard her she touched something in me, she connected with me even though I was amongst hundreds in the room. She connected with me. Now that's being real.

This is just who I am and I like it!

Be real and vulnerable.

Being Real in a High Achiever's Business World

Some of the high achievers amongst us could also learn to take a little more time to be real. A lot of high achievers have an element of overwhelm and a drive to constantly keep going to achieve perfection. Not only perfection but a lot of it. They push themselves and take on a huge workload to be the best in the office – to prove their worth to their bosses and the world. What is interesting is that the perfectionists of this world are actually constantly focused on imperfection. It is only through that focus that they see what is not perfect. What we focus on is what we create, so more often than not the perfectionists of this world are actually experts at creating imperfection – ironic isn't it? Often their deep belief is that they are not worth anything without what they have produced. In a very potent presentation from a high achiever talking about this self worth, she said, "I have had to learn that I am loved not for what I do but for who I am." This is an essence of self worth. Being real can help balance out the need to achieve, the 'being loved for what I do', and get us to relax into who we are and thus reduce the overwhelm.

Living in Spain has taught me to notice when I get into this space of overwhelm. My past pattern would be to set myself many tight and normally impossible targets. In doing so I would set up a time of stress and worry. However, I now live on the Mediterranean coast of Southern Spain – the sea is just outside my window, the culture is that of mañana – no hurry; tomorrow. Even if I want to have things happen immediately it simply isn't possible. I learnt this very early in my time here. I was hurrying down the street (rushing to get something done!) and passed a Spanish acquaintance. Back in the UK this would have merited a brief 'hello' as I moved on by. In Spain you stop, give the traditional two-cheek kiss, and talk for at least five minutes, probably more. Nothing is more important in Spain than people. In this laid-back atmosphere I have been forced to take a look at my target-setting and can now see that it is all choice. All these targets are self-imposed deadlines. Some necessary, some not so much. In these situations it is really easy to feel annoyed with God – 'what's happening here – I've got so much work to do – give me a break!' Spain, and its culture of the tortoise rather than the hare has taught me to stand back. From this I can see that it is all my own creation. It is all in my mind. Why?

Because at these times I'm no longer being real. I am focusing on what I feel about what is happening rather than what is actually happening. As a good friend used to say to me after I ranted on about a situation and my take on it, "Well that's the story, now what's actually happening?" We get so good at the story we lose sight of the facts. With most of my tasks it was not that it actually mattered if something was finished by today or tomorrow, it was that I would feel better if it was. Another thing ticked off my list. All this gave me was a feeling of achievement, but even that in itself was false.

Living life spiritually – applied spirituality – is about being practical, being honest with yourself at all times. How often have you found yourself in this type of situation, a dozen projects to finish, not enough time and two other people wanting your time too? We end up in people-pleasing mode rather than being-real mode. How can we change this? How can we do the tasks in our day, achieve what we want and not get into overwhelm?

Approach everything you do with an attitude of being real. To learn that we are loved for who we are, we have to take the risk of consciously breaking the stressed achiever's pattern of behaviour. When setting priorities, be real with them. Look at the practicalities of the situation. Learn to say no, both to yourself, 'No, I won't give into the habit of pleasing others in detriment to myself'. And, 'No' to others who push you beyond what is humanly and humanely possible. If we take this level of responsibility we cannot blame others if we feel overwhelmed.

To help you start this process, look at all the tasks that are creating the feeling of overwhelm and list them in order of importance. Now ask yourself, what can be dropped until a later date? What can have a lesser amount of time allotted to it? What has to be done now? If you take a step back and look you will see a pattern of how you create this overwhelm, both in the workplace and in your personal life. Not only could you prioritise yourself out of it, but also you could stop it happening in the first place. Overwhelm is created in our lives when we are so focused on what has to happen in the future that we feel unable to take one step forward. By bringing our focus back to now, prioritising now, overwhelm decreases magically.

Most importantly, do the tasks to the best of your ability, but remember that it is part of the play, God's play, and enjoy it. Stop trying to get life done, that's not being real. Learn to enjoy whatever the task is before you, rather than getting it done so you can move on. We wish life away like that, and lose the gift of the present moment. We can realise our divinity in any moment in any task whatever our like or dislike of it. If you are totally focused on the end of the journey you will forget to enjoy the view along the way.

Being Real, Being Inspired

When we are not being real we can become stressed. I had a friend who recently was asked by a local council to give a talk on stress management. He told me that when he was preparing his normal presentation, it began to feel very heavy, not at all inspired. He sat back and took a breath and meditated for a while on why he felt this way. Suddenly he got the hit that actually he didn't want to talk about stress management at all. By talking about stress management he felt that he was acknowledging that stress was acceptable and that it just had to be managed. He wanted to talk about being stress free. How stress is a mind, body, spirit issue and that the best way is to address it as such.

So he winged it and gave the talk he wanted to give rather than the one that had been requested. He was being real both with himself and with those who came to listen. He even told me that instead of standing behind the podium, which gave the feeling of authority and safety that he was used to, he came out front and close up to the audience. This dropped the barrier, physically and energetically, he became more real and it became a dialogue rather than a lecture.

He said that he had been feeling stressed when he tried to write the original talk but felt light and flowing when he followed his inspiration to talk about being stress free. As a bonus he got the best feedback from the audience that he had ever received and many more people wanted to take his ideas further. He said that he felt that he was serving some higher purpose and that the inspiration came from his Self rather than his self. He just had to get over his fear of people not liking what he did (not being loved) and follow his truth.

How often have we denied the inspiration within us and not honoured ourselves? How often have we half-heartedly sat in a meeting or put in the minimum effort required for fear of speaking out? If we are going to live life to the full, if we are going to participate fully then we need to be in integrity with ourselves at all times. We need to be real. This may mean disappointing or upsetting 'others'. But on the larger picture we know there is no 'other', and difficult and odd as it may seem we need to start living life as though everybody knows and understands this. If people choose to become upset because we follow our highest truth then so be it. But – and this is really important – to be a real human being is to follow our truth, our highest.

I have found that when I follow my truth it more often than not works out. If I communicate from my heart, with total honesty, no beating about the bush, and definitely no excuses – just plain compassionate truth, then those who I think will be upset/disappointed actually are fine. They hear a Being being honest and loving and the God within them responds. Truth and Integrity always comes through.

In business, speak from the heart.

Why is it that we are so frightened to speak our truth – to say things as they are? Why do we recourse to excuses, especially in business or commerce? I was once working for a training department within an organisation and I had made the mistake of inviting someone to a training who had actually been taken off the invite list. It was decided that this person now had to be uninvited from the training. In the ensuing conversation everyone tried to think of the excuse I could use. What could I say that would make it ok? After this was talked around for a while I simply said 'let's say the truth'. Let's tell him that it was a mistake and although his name had been put forward it was decided not to invite him. The reason for this was because he needed to work on his understanding of certain principles before he moved into this area of work. It was not a reflection on him as a person but of where he was in this training cycle. To most people in the meeting this seemed a very strange and new suggestion but it was agreed. I called him up and explained the situation, I spoke honestly, with love and compassion, I was real. He heard every word, knew it to be the truth and totally accepted the situation. He also thanked us for our honesty and he then went on to study the required area and take a later seminar and is now a very respected team member. That would never have happened had we made up an excuse.

We only learn this by taking the plunge and doing it. No amount of theory is going to show you the immense benefits of being real in your own life. Practise makes perfect and we can achieve much by practising this level of realness. People are drawn to truth – if we increase our 'being real level' in our lives, whether it be in our personal lives or in business, the benefits will show. Our relationships will deepen as we let that special someone in and see us for who we truly are. If we are single we will begin to attract real people into our lives, our beacon of realness will act like a light that will beam out and touch others of a similar light. In business we will gain a reputation of being honest, open and trustworthy, all invaluable in a world where trust and respect are desired, but not always possible. And, not only that, we will feel more alive than ever before.

Being Real Energetically

As we become more real in our outer lives we also become aware of being real energetically. I read a passage on karma, the universal law that states that as you sow so shall you reap, which related to our energetic realness. It said, 'One thing is certain – how we actually treat others and not how we think we treat them, will come back to us as karma.' As I contemplated this sentence many things came to mind. One is the insidious nature of our ego when it makes us think that we are being nice, kind and caring but, in fact, behind those words are anger, resentment and blame. Another is the power of words. All sound is a vibration and those vibrations that we send out all the time with our words are what affects the people they collide with. The Sanskrit language is a perfect demonstration of this. Each original word and root of the words carries the vibrational energy of what it describes. I have witnessed a Hindu fire ceremony in which the Brahmin priests, chanting Sanskrit mantras, created fire with the words. Once you realise the incredible power of the vibration of our words you begin to see the implications they can have.

However, it is subtler than that – the words may say one thing but the actual energy behind the words affects people too. How often have you been with someone who is acting as if nothing is wrong, but you can feel that in fact they are very agitated for some reason? You ask them what's wrong and they say, "nothing, I'm fine" and you simply know that that is not the case. This is a clear indication of when our words do not match our energy. When we are not being energetically real.

I'm sure that almost all of you have heard of the Hawaiian greeting 'Aloha'. You often hear it in the movies when someone arrives on the islands and they are greeted with a garland of flowers. Nowadays it is written above hotel entrances as a greeting, it is used in every place a tourist goes, it has become the Hawaiian symbol. However, I read recently that there is a much deeper meaning to this word. It does signify a greeting, a farewell or an expression of love, but the word itself can be broken into two pieces. 'Alo' means 'in the presence of' and 'ha' means 'God'. In the olden days the word was only spoken consciously with love and truth, it was spoken with a realness behind it and to speak it thoughtlessly without love was the equivalent to lying. This conscious greeting is one example of being real energetically.

How can we be aware of this, how can we be sure that we are not affecting someone adversely with our words, our energy? Committing to being real, being congruent is one step, constantly checking in with our intention. I can remember one incident when I was getting frustrated. My point of view as well as my way of having things done was not being agreed with. In other words I was not getting my own way! However, at one point I decided to stop arguing and allow the other person to do what they wanted. I thought all right, just be supportive and let go and see what happens. I truly thought in that moment that I was being spiritual when in fact it was the opposite.

Why? Because I was saying one thing and still feeling another. Our egos are very tricky. It will become the chameleon whenever it thinks that it will benefit. So we say the right words and seem to be doing the right supportive action when actually, almost subconsciously, we are holding on to the opposite view and energetically condemning the person and situation.

When I replayed this situation in my mind, I saw myself push down the judgmental thought and choose the supportive one, but I did not totally mean it. And this is where it is so important to be extra vigilant. I then reread the sentence "how we *actually* treat others and not how we *think* we treat them." Looking at what had occurred I could see how I had not been real energetically.

I asked myself what could I have done had I had this awareness then? Remember: It is always great to learn by hindsight, when you see something that you wish to change, play back the situation and ask yourself – with this new understanding how could I have been more real?

I saw that I could have paused and simply asked myself how do I feel in this moment? It doesn't take long because these heart-felt questions are answered instantly. I then could have spoken with honesty and truth about how I felt and, most importantly, with compassion and without charge. I could have acknowledged that this was different from the other person's view. By speaking out clearly I would be honouring my truth. It would then be possible to have said that, although I believe that it could be done differently, we can agree to differ. I could have both physically and energetically stepped back. From that standpoint I could have chosen to really support them in their decision. Nothing about the (physical) outcome would have changed. However, the subtle, energetic outcome would be different. My input both physically and energetically would have been congruent and in harmony and therefore creating harmony in life. The simple act of speaking out, of being real in the moment, would have changed it totally.

Not only do we have to watch our own energy in our interactions with others, we also need to be aware of our energetic reactions to places as well as situations and people. Have you felt uncomfortable when you have walked into a place, a feeling of 'something not quite right' and not been able to put a finger on it? This is our energy telling us something is amiss. A lot of the time we will not know what it is that is not quite right but if we are being real with ourselves then we need to take note of what we are feeling. Sometimes we may feel the need to leave, other times simply to be aware of what is going on around us and to protect ourselves if necessary.

Our energetic body is like an early warning system; it picks up energies of places and people and gives us feedback. As we become more sensitive we notice it more. To begin with it may be the extremes we pick up, when we walk into a beautiful home where the people living there are happy and fun we feel light, and we want to be there. But as our level of realness becomes more refined we pick up energies that are fleeting, more subtle. Our responsibility is to listen and act on the feedback we get.

A friend a mine tells a story of a tempestuous relationship in which, on the first evening, when she saw her date's feet as she came down the stairs, (her energy entered her energetic field) she thought, 'there's something wrong, this is never going to work'. She ignored this energetic hit and they went on to have a stormy relationship which, when it eventually ended, was a relief for them both. Had she been real, listened to her energetic feedback, she would have had one date and said goodnight. Instead she had nine months of emotional upheaval.

Sometimes we pick up the energy even before it arrives...

Being real energetically can sometimes not feel logical. How can we make decisions on a funny feeling inside, something we can't even put a name to? Again, practise, start with the small stuff and expand from there. Practise following the feelings and life will become spontaneous and rich in its experiences. We need to become aware of our energy, remember to check in with ourselves. As with all things, first set the intention, next is action. Make the commitment to take notice of these energetic hits. If you feel yourself in an odd situation stop, breathe and experience what you are feeling. The more you honour and follow them the more attuned you will become. As you review your day and practise gratitude for all that happened, add some gratitude for the times you noticed your energetic messages. By being grateful for them you create a positive feedback that encourages your subconscious to notice them more. At the same time we will begin to trust our energy and learn to manage, be true to it and live life in congruence between the outer and inner world. It becomes your second nature.

Being real is a daily practise and one that we can deepen until we reach that state of complete realness, true connection. It is the taking of responsibility in our lives, our interactions with others and generally how we operate in this realm. If we are real with ourselves as well as with others we can no longer blame anyone for anything, not even God, and, we will be Remembering Perfection.

Tips

- To gain an insight into your own situation, and to start being real to yourself, it is useful to ask yourself what is happening around you. See what is being mirrored to you through your relationships, your work situation, things that happen around you. Then ask yourself, 'how does this apply to me and what I do in my life?' For further insight into how real you are, you can also talk with someone you trust who knows you well and see if they can shed any light.

- When you're faced with the choice of being real or hiding and feel nervous, one support is to remember that this nervousness is simply energy. Know that this is the energy of the universe – the Shakti. When you feel this energy, know that you are in touch with the God within and are totally supported in being real. Let the energy flow through you, feel it and know it to be a positive force.

- When you start to feel unworthy and/or if you have a tendency to judge yourself for what you achieve, remind yourself that you are truly loved, not for what you do but for who you are.

- When you get caught up in overwhelm remember to look at what is happening rather than what you are feeling about what is happening. Ask yourself, 'Well that's the story, now what's actually happening?' Once you see the difference you can then become practical, become real. From this standpoint you can prioritise. Look at all the tasks that are creating the feeling of overwhelm and list them in order of importance. What can be dropped until a later date? What can have a lesser amount of time allotted to it? What has to be done now? It is your choice.

- Learn to say No. No is as big a part of being real as Yes. It also enhances your self-worth.

- Stop trying to get life done, that's not being real. Learn to enjoy whatever the task is before you, rather than getting it done so you can move on. Notice the view as you journey forward.

- Follow your inspiration, it comes from your Self.

- Be congruent with your energy; make sure your energy matches your words.

- Learn through hindsight. When you identify something that you wish to change, play back the situation and ask yourself – with this new understanding how could I have been more real?

Contemplation

Give yourself at least half an hour for this contemplation. If you have a place within your home where you meditate use this space or, if not, just find somewhere quiet where you will not be disturbed. Have your journal or a notebook handy.

Before you start this contemplation identify one idea or phrase that stood out for you in this chapter. It might be being honest with yourself, or getting real about what is actually happening in your life. You now need to devise a question for you to contemplate. For example it could be, 'in what way could I be more honest with myself?' Or 'what does being real with myself mean?' Settle on whatever question feels right for you, something that will give you insight into the idea.

Get into a comfortable position and gently relax your body by taking some deep breaths. Breathe into any area of your body that holds tension and as you breathe out feel the tension flowing out with your breath. Once you feel relaxed bring your breathing back to your normal rhythm and simply focus on your breath for a few minutes. At this point invite Grace into your contemplation in whatever way seems appropriate for you. Now ask yourself the question you wish to contemplate. Ask it three times and then simply sit and see what comes to mind. If you find your mind wandering simply bring it back to the question. After sitting with the question for a while pick up your pen and begin to write. Let the answer flow, do not censor it, stop it or word-craft it. Simply allow your wisdom to emerge. Once you have finished sit quietly for a moment and acknowledge the wisdom and insight received.

CHAPTER FOUR

Creating Reality

Anything is possible when we truly believe in it.

We each create our own reality whether we believe it or not. Everything in our world is connected; all things exist on an energetic level. We are therefore part of the creative process. The power of creation starts in energy, the divine, and moves down the vibratory levels from inspiration, through thought and finally action. As you think so you are. There are different ways of creating reality, whether it be a physical outcome or simply an attitude to a situation. However, in the end it is a matter of where your mind is, the emotions that that brings up in you and how you feel about it. Is your mind present? What fantasies is it creating right now? Are you even aware of the stories it is telling you? What beliefs are ruling your reality right now? What emotions are you feeling because of your thoughts? In this chapter we will explore the power of our minds and how we truly do create our own reality.

The Energy of Creation

Creating reality in its fullest version indicates that we can create anything we wish for in our lives. All things are energy on some level. The science of quantum physics is based around these theories. The film, *What the Bleep Do We Know*, a part-documentary, part-story, has many respected physicists, scientists and spiritual teachers talking exactly about this energetic source of everything.

In the film, John Hagelin Ph.D. talks about the deepest level of truth uncovered by both science and philosophy and explains that it is the fundamental truth of the unity. He goes on to explain that at the deepest sub-nuclear level of our reality, you and I are literally one. Fred Alan Wolfe Ph.D. expands that thought, explaining that what makes up things are not more things, what makes up things are ideas, concepts and information.

Lynne McTaggart, in her book *The Field*, also investigates the energetic source of all things in the Universe. She talks about how science has begun to prove what is written in spiritual literature – that there is an underlying life force or energy field connecting all things, the Zero Point Field. In a nutshell the only thing that differentiates an apple from a chair is the density and level of vibration. All things are connected through this uninterrupted energetic stream. In fact, all things are this energy, there is nothing else. This energy is God, is Perfection. If this is the case then our thoughts are also energy. Here lies the starting place of creation. As you think so you are, and so the world is.

There is, however, a caveat to this theory. We can only create when we are unattached to the outcome of our desire, when our thoughts are in their purest form without any egoic hangers on. In other words, if we have any negative emotional attachment to what we are trying to create then we will block, or at least slow down, the creation with that emotional charge. All creation is energetic and our emotions are one part of that energy. If our emotions are not in line with the feeling we would get by realising our desire it is like a tug of war, one side fighting the other and no movement – or only very slow movement is possible. Another block to creation is our fear. We have no fear of creating something insignificant like a parking space. It doesn't cost us anything energetically and we do not have to deal with a past issue or belief to 'pay' for it. We do not see any significant consequences to creating a parking space. Larger acts of creation are expensive energetically as they require us not to be afraid of the consequences of creation. More often than not the larger creation holds change for us and that can be scary. If we truly did create change in our lives then that would have an influence on all areas of our life as well as on the lives of those around us. To really create our reality we need to be free of the emotional fears, beliefs and blocks that rule our subconscious world. When we have done this we can create anything we want. As Caroline Myss talks about in her seminars, life is a paradox – what's scary is safe and what's safe is scary. Life is the journey of becoming reversed. Our ability to create is directly linked to our ability to trust this paradox, jump in the deep end and face ourselves in the process.

We are constantly creating our reality even if we don't realise it. This is quite a difficult idea for some people. When we first encounter it we don't want to believe it, for if we did we'd have to say that we have created everything in our lives, both 'good' and 'bad'. But once we allow ourselves to accept this truth then there is amazing potential. What we have created with our minds we can now create anew and different if we so choose. This is why it is so important that we become vigilant of what our minds are doing. If we want to create something but have an attachment to it, a fear it will not happen or a lack of belief in the possibility it will, then we will create that lack, that which we fear. Our emotions are the turbo charger to creation and if we focus our emotions on our fears then that is what we get, the fear. We can see this in the downward spiral that some people get caught in. For example, if money is tight and we are constantly focusing on our lack of money, isn't it true that often yet another bill will land on the mat?

We need to increase our ability of being aware of what our minds think at all times. This can seem quite overwhelming, how on earth can we be vigilant about every single thought? We can't, and because we can't, we have an inner guidance system that, when we listen to it, will inform us if we are thinking positive thoughts. This system is our emotions. Simply put, if we are thinking happy, positive, life-affirming thoughts then we feel good. When we feel good we are thinking the kind of thoughts that will create what we want. Conversely, if we think negative, fearful, angry thoughts then we won't feel very good. This is a wake-up call to notice our thoughts and choose to change them.

Once we become aware of what our minds are thinking we can start to focus on what we want rather than what we don't want.

We can start to see abundance and focus on money coming towards us, on having rather than not having. At this point we can start to feel how it will be once this abundance comes into our lives, it is these feelings that act as a magnet and draw in the experience. As we begin to live it; act as if it is already in our lives, start feeling wealthy within, these thoughts attract the reality. As Mike Dooley, author and speaker from Totally Unique Thoughts always says, thoughts become things.

There is also another reason to be vigilant around our thoughts. In the Bartholomew book, *From the Heart of a Gentle Brother*, we are asked to think about the concept of harmlessness. Are all our thoughts harmless? In this world, one of the reasons we do not instantly create with our thoughts is because often they are not always harmless. This can be both towards ourselves as well as others. Think about a simple statement said in haste, for example, 'I wish I were dead'. What if we did instantly create reality with our thoughts? What outcome would that one statement have? This idea of harmlessness brought me up short when I read it. I suddenly had a vision of all the things my thoughts could have created if they were instant, some funnier than others, especially my comments about Spanish drivers! As we move towards creating our reality we need to become aware of what our minds think.

We each have our own beliefs and blocks. Whether we feel we deserve something or not will have an effect on what we create in our lives as much as a belief that we are capable of achieving a goal or not. Some people truly believe without a doubt that if they are supposed to do something then they will receive the support they need instantly. A friend of mine was walking the Camino de Santiago de Compostela, a pilgrimage path in Northern Spain, and her focus was about having her needs met. She had been taking a look at her life and had realised that she held back on a lot of her dreams because of subconscious survival fear. She began to see that if she could deeply know that her basic needs would always be met then she would live her life more fully. One day on the pilgrimage she wanted to buy some bread for her picnic on the walk but could not find any. She decided that she would simply trust that she would be taken care of, know that food would come to her when she needed it and set out on the next stage of her walk though open countryside. Around lunch time she stopped, tired and hungry and just sat down in the shade of an old olive tree. As she dozed in the sun imagine her joy and excitement as a van drove out of nowhere and there, in the middle of the countryside, stopped beside her. It was a bread van. Lunch had arrived!

As she told me the story I got the feeling that it didn't even seem like a miracle, but was simply a result of an absolute knowing that her needs would be met. Her unattached, pure thought, along with the positive emotion that accompanied the thought, had created the reality. That positive emotion; the inner guidance from within that she was on the right wavelength, the good, happy feeling that she felt when she 'knew', was an integral part of the creation. Not only did she know it for real, but she also felt good as she thought that thought. The 'how' she didn't need to know, only that it would somehow happen. In these situations we need to be aware of our 'how' expectations. Had she set off expecting her problem to be solved in a specific way (i.e. if she had thought she would be given some bread by another walker on the path) she would have blocked the flow of universal creativity by locking her energy into a specific way the goal could be achieved.

This is also a very important part of the creative process, leaving the 'hows' alone. It is not our job to know how something is going to happen, our job is simply the 'what'. If we start limiting the Universe as to how it can deliver our dream then we are really slowing the process down. If my friend had only allowed the Universe to bring lunch via another walker on the path then the bread van simply could not have driven past her. By leaving the 'hows' alone her simple knowing was answered in a much more fun and miraculous way.

Creating reality is actually a process of co-creation, between us and Source. We can co-create our reality in any area of our lives, sometimes the miraculous type and sometimes purely in our minds by choosing our attitude to a situation. The level of creativity is up to us. In this chapter we will be looking at how we can co-create the physical reality in our lives. How we can influence what happens through looking at our beliefs and expectations, and how we sabotage what we think we want. In the following chapter we will investigate the metaphysical side of reality, how our attitude to a situation can create a reality, the power of our mind in any given situation as well as the power of fear and how we can work our way through it.

Beliefs; Conscious and Subconscious

Like many people, I played enthusiastically with the idea of creating my reality when I first came across it. I became very good at creating a parking space outside Barclays bank in Minehead. I would simply ask for and visualise a space. Every time without fail a space would open up as I drove round the corner. Hey, neat, I would think. I see now that the key to this was my non-attachment, my attitude of it being a game rather than a life-and-death need. It was fun and I felt good doing it. Once again that energy of fun and playfulness had acted as a magnet. Somehow it seemed reasonable to create parking spaces and I totally believed it was possible. I have spoken with many people who can do parking spaces easily, but the big things in life – well that's a different matter. It's easier to believe it is possible with parking than, for example, creating a perfect job. Why?

Our beliefs play a large part in the creation of our world. It is not just our conscious beliefs that we create, it is our subconscious ones too. These subconscious beliefs are the limiting decisions we hold in our unconscious mind. Decisions made in the spur of the moment during a significant emotional event. Because of the intensity of the emotion we sometimes read a limiting meaning into what was said or done. For example if we had lost a friend when we were young because they moved away, but it wasn't explained to us why they had left, we might have supposed at that young age that people you loved leave. This then becomes a limiting decision that clouds all future relationships. It might not have even been an event that happened to us, it could simply be something we have picked up from those around us, or even those carried from other lifetimes.

Conscious beliefs are often different, even contradictory, to the subconscious ones. However, these limiting decisions can actually be more powerful. How do I know this? Because I have created things in my life that I did not consciously want or believe in. When I first moved to Spain I thought that it would be possible to set up a new business quite quickly. However, despite my belief, this was not the case. As I explored my belief system I realised that my limiting decision was opposing. I believed that if things came to me then I was lucky – not deserving. In fact, I thought that it was pretty amazing that things came to me at all in spite of the fact that I was not deserving. This subconscious belief was very strong – stronger than the conscious belief, and it was that belief that created my reality. Things, therefore, did not come easily.

Expectations are also beliefs that play a part. The ego uses many sneaky ways for us to think one thing and create another. As I contemplated my belief about deserving things, I realised that although I thought that I would (note the future tense there) create the new business, my expectation was that it would take a long time. I actually had two things working against creating what I wanted. A limiting decision and an expectation.

Even as we create our reality the ego finds other ways to sabotage the process – if it can't totally stop your change then it will do whatever it can to slow down the outcome. It is rather like a child who tries every ruse they can think of to delay going to bed. There might be an inevitability about it, but they sure as hell are going to drag it out as long as possible. Why is that? Why does the ego sabotage the process?

It can be quite helpful to think of our ego as the recalcitrant child. It is very clever at getting its own way. It sees our attempts at change as a threat to its existence. And it's right, it is a threat, for when you master your life, when you live in an awareness of God at all times, your ego is no longer in charge.

Ramakrishna, a highly respected Indian saint who lived in the 1800s, saw the ego as the coachman and the Soul as the owner of a coach and horses. Because the coachman (ego) cannot see the owner of the coach (Soul) sitting quietly inside he believes he is totally in charge. However, as the owner gradually but firmly makes himself known, the coachman, maybe reluctantly at first, relinquishes and drops the fantasy of control and eventually becomes content with the role of servant. It is the same with us. Our ego is sure that it totally runs our show, but gradually as we become more aware of our spiritual nature, our Soul, we can choose to come from our heart rather than be at the mercy of our egoistic responses. When this happens, the ego becomes a useful and essential tool for getting things done in the world.

It takes time for this process to evolve but evolve it does. When you see what game the ego is playing with one of your newly discovered beliefs, treat it like that recalcitrant child – be firm and choose what you want to have happen. For me, even after I saw that my belief of not deserving was not true, my ego would still bring up old memories that reinforced my old belief. My job was to notice this and choose to think differently.

Beliefs rule us until we see them for what they are. The good news is that they can be changed, Neuro-linguistic Programming (NLP) is one very effective method that we will explore. However, we need to unearth our limiting beliefs or decisions to be able to change them. One illuminating exercise to do, and I encourage you to try this, is to write down all your beliefs in a particular context, e.g. beliefs about relationships. Sit down with a paper and pen and write down anything that comes to mind. It may take a few days to unearth them all, but let them flow without judging or censoring them. Commons ones are, 'I have to work very hard and be very lucky to succeed', 'I'll never be able to lose weight' 'I'm not good enough', 'I'll always be alone', 'I'm always unlucky', 'Life's not fair'. What are your beliefs? Once you've got them all down, take a look at the list and write next to each belief the name of the person from whom it came. Mother, father, teacher, friend, priest and so on – name each one. For example, my belief about success coming slowly came from a feeling I picked up from my family. I have heard that you had to work hard and long for good things to come. Now the interesting thing is that this might never have even been said but it was my interpretation and that's what stuck. Most people find it very surprising to see that many of their beliefs have not come from their own life experience. They have been living their life and making decisions based on certain beliefs that are not even theirs.

The next step is to go through the list again and cross out any beliefs that you do not actually believe in. Sound contradictory? Yes, in some ways it is, but it is also revealing to see that some beliefs we thought were set in stone are actually not true for us now. At this point we can make the conscious choice not to act from them any more. This is a very freeing process. It allows us to become very clear as to what we can now choose to believe.

It is often at this time that many people realise that some of the religious beliefs they have carried with them for years also are not their own. More and more people are questioning the vengeful God that is portrayed in some religions and that was possibly introduced to us in our childhood. Now can be the time to start finding out for ourselves just exactly what do we believe when it comes to our spiritual life. I recently looked up spiritual in the dictionary and it said, 'relating to the Spirit, relating to the Soul'. At the same time I looked up religious – amongst many things it said, 'believing in a religion, controlled by a religion, unquestioning'. I ask you, as you look at your list of beliefs, to ask yourself whose beliefs they are. If they are not your truth, not your experience, then I suggest you drop them from your operating perimeter and start living an empowered life from your truth – and only your truth.

It may take time to change some of the deep-seated beliefs that you've held for so many years and in some cases you may want professional help. If you feel that your belief has a deep emotional charge, I would recommend working with a therapist or NLP practitioner to create a safe space for you to deal with whatever comes up.

Your ego will want to keep running these programs for as long as possible and one of the ego's disguises is the saboteur. This is the subconscious program that runs in the shadows, the voice in your head, the inner critic. How often have you had a good idea only to find that judging voice inside telling you how silly it is? The inner critic originally developed to keep us safe. As children we picked up very quickly what kind of behaviour was favoured by our parents and authority figures. For example, if we were told the old maxim, 'children are to be seen and not heard' we might have a critical voice that stops us voicing our opinion. Even though the situation that gave us this belief came from when we were young, it might still hold true today until we shine a light on it and see that it no longer has any authority.

The saboteur can be very convincing, especially when we are about to go against its advice. It will come up with better and better arguments for not doing something. For example, if someone was thinking of speaking up for the first time in a work situation, it will bring up all the other times it hasn't worked. 'Remember ten years ago' it will say, 'when you spoke up in that awful job you had and got shouted down. You don't want that to happen again.' What it won't remind you is that it was your first job, and you were working with a group of incredibly competitive people who would have shouted down anyone who came up with an idea they didn't have. The ego will bring out the saboteur voice whenever it senses that you might be about to flout one of your old beliefs.

Caroline Myss, in her book *Sacred Contracts*, talks about how we all have twelve personal archetypal energies but that four are common to us all. One is the saboteur. Our egos use this energy to magnify our fears and low self-esteem to stop us moving forward in our lives. It preys upon our insecurities and does its best to hold us where we are. There is, however, a positive side to this archetype, as to all of them. When we befriend this archetype and face it in our lives, making it an ally, it will begin to show you when you are about to sabotage a situation. That, in turn, gives you the power to make a different choice.

So one of the keys to creating reality is belief. If you don't believe that something is possible, no amount of positive thinking will bring it to you. Nevertheless, affirmations are still a useful tool to aid the work with changing beliefs, especially in unearthing the saboteur. I used to have a great resistance to affirmations. I'd labelled them 'New Age' and completely disregarded them. How could I possibly state something as true, right in that moment, when I knew that it wasn't? I could see for myself that what I was affirming wasn't real. So, for many years I ignored the possibility of affirmations, all the while believing I create my reality. Bit paradoxical? No not necessarily, just backwards.

I could totally believe that I created my reality especially when things went wrong. Something negative would happen and I'd sit there and say, 'see, told you so, I've been thinking that that might happen and it did.' I had created my fears once again, something we will explore later. We are all very good at creating our fears, but often fail to make the connection that the same method can be used to create our dreams. Affirmations can be either positive or negative. Once I realised that, I could see how we can work with our belief system through affirmations.

Unearthing the Saboteur

When I started to work with my belief of not-deserving I started to use an affirmation of 'I am grateful that my efforts are always acknowledged and rewarded. I am in demand.' This affirmation unearthed the saboteur with great affect!

To start to unearth the saboteur I now use affirmations for myself and with my coaching clients. Affirmations can bring up a lot of old issues, so be prepared for this if it happens. They are great for unearthing those pesky subconscious beliefs that block things happening. The first thing is to word the affirmation in positive, present tense words. I am… I have… I live… whatever it is you want to work on. Choose your words carefully. Affirmations should have an emotional element too, this can be the gratitude, 'I am grateful that …' or a feeling like satisfaction, joy, fun.

When you have finalised the wording of your affirmation, split your page into two columns. Write the affirmation out in the left-hand column and then write out whatever that inner critic, judge, parent, saboteur voice says to the contrary. This is very important as it is this unearthing of the saboteur that begins the process of moving away from the old belief and creating the new. See what it says, give it full voice, feel the emotion behind that voice. Is it angry, sad, hurt, defeated, in a rage? What do you physically feel as you hear what it has to say? How do you feel about the voice behind the voice, whose is it? Can you see what it was that happened that created this voice and this belief? Many of our beliefs are created from others, through others. Most likely, at the time they were given to us, it was to protect and keep us safe in this world. But what you were given then does not necessarily serve you now. Write down everything that comes up at this stage, it will all be relevant as you work to change the belief. It will also alert you in the future when the saboteur is about to influence you once again.

Another way to use your affirmation is to take some time each day to visualise it. Our imagination is very powerful and a useful tool for creation. As you repeat your affirmation in your mind actually see the situation play out before your eyes. For example, if you wish to act differently with someone who normally makes you angry and intolerant, visualise the circumstances and see yourself being calm, loving and supportive. Really get into how it feels, use this positive feeling to attract new circumstances towards you, feel what the outcome of this new way of being will be. As we play these scenarios through our mind we energetically create change as well as set up new neural pathways, which in turn will be sparked when presented with an opportunity to act differently.

Visualisation is a very powerful tool and demonstrates the power of the mind. Athletes have used it successfully for many years. In one experiment, athletes were wired up to sensors and asked to visualise running a 100 metres. As they did so their muscles fired up in sequence as though they were actually running – this is the power of the mind, it simply didn't know the difference between the actual running of the race and the visualisation. Using visualisation for creating something new in your life harnesses this power of the mind and focuses it on the opportunities that you may not have seen before.

Neuro-linguistic Programming is based on the neural pathways we have in our brain and body. Each time we think a particular thought a chemical reaction occurs in the brain between two synapses – like a spark between two wires. If we constantly think a thought again and again – like a belief we may have – this neural pathway gets strong and it is very difficult to think differently. In other words it is hard to send our thoughts down different wires. Becoming aware of our thoughts can have a big effect on our lives as we begin to focus our minds and energy toward what we want rather than what we do not want. NLP processes are designed to go back to the first event that caused us to think the thought that created a decision to be made, which in turn became a limiting belief. By addressing the moment the decision was made, the sponsoring decision, it is like cutting the end pearl off a string of pearls, all the others can fall off too and beliefs can be changed.

As I used my affirmation I began to see that situations in my past gave me the feeling of not ever deserving or getting what I wish for. I began to see my limiting decision that was made many moons ago. I saw that everyone else got their wish but me. One situation that came to mind was a time when I wanted to change schools and do my A levels at my brother's old school that had just started taking girls. I had worshipped the school for years, each visit to the open day reinforced this huge desire to be part of this community of great people. When I was accepted I was over the moon. However, two weeks later, the place was cancelled as my current headmistress said I wouldn't pass my O levels. I can remember the incredible crushing feeling of disappointment and accompanying it was the 'well of course, it's obvious, I couldn't be that lucky to go to such a place'. Even when I got the grades it was too late to salvage the place at the school, yet another thing I didn't deserve – a second chance.

I could have experienced this whole episode differently, but I already held the belief that I didn't deserve good things. This came from my take I had on things that happened in life. What

I made certain circumstances mean. Being rather younger than my brothers and sister I naturally didn't get to do everything they did. I created a world in my mind in which I was left out, didn't deserve to be a part of things. Interestingly, when I speak with those who knew me as a child, their experience of my childhood is one of the total opposite. They tell me that I was incredibly spoilt and got to have and do everything I wanted that was possible! We each choose our own reality, it is just our individual take on a situation.

In fact our individual take on the situation is the only thing that has power. We take on beliefs like sponges and often they can come from something that is a misunderstanding, or a strong emotional event as we looked at before. They can also be something that was said to us and we hear something different. For example, I thought for years that I was a bit dumb. I passed exams but felt I had to work incredibly hard and never thought that I would excel. When I failed to get into my brother's old school it was just a confirmation of what I knew to be true.

It came as shock therefore, when I took an IQ test in a company I worked for that employed over 100 people, that I was number two in the whole company. Even then I still didn't get it. Years later I was contemplating this belief and I cast my mind back to a time when I felt dumb. What came to me was a time – and I must have been about eleven – when my father said to me, "it doesn't matter if you pass or fail as long as you do your best." Here was I, going in for an exam, and he was encouraging me and trying to take the pressure off. Or so he thought. What I heard was, "we don't expect you to pass". From that one comment a false sponsoring belief was sown.

There is a great demonstration of this type of situation, where one person's reality is totally different to another's, in Milan Kundera's novel, *Ignorance.* In the book two characters meet again after many years. For her it is reconciliation of huge importance, this man was her great, unconsummated love. He didn't even recognise her. They lived this encounter coming from totally different places, assumptions were made, decisions taken on those assumptions. It is a perfect demonstration of how often we think we are on the same page when actually we aren't even in the same book! How often have we caught ourselves making decisions based on what we find out later to be a totally false belief? And, when we do, are we willing to address those beliefs and change our reality?

As you do these affirmations and unearth the sponsoring beliefs it is crucial to get to the bottom of those beliefs. You need to get to the root of the blockage in your psyche and work from there. If you feel worried about digging into the past unsupported, work with a coach, counsellor or NLP practitioner specifically around your beliefs. To start, take a look at where you are in your life. Which area is not flowing, which area do you feel unfulfilled in? It is these areas of unfulfilled dreams that you can choose to work with. So often we don't allow ourselves to have big dreams, big wishes. As I work with clients it is often the case that once people see that they can create things in their life their dreams expand as their limiting beliefs are disempowered.

If, for example, you would like to create more abundance and wealth in your life, you could start with an affirmation, 'I am grateful that I consistently create wealth in my life". As you use this affirmation, start to notice the saboteur voice, the unconscious belief that works against this. Identify it, the source of where it came from, then dis-empower it. How? By addressing the belief at its core, the first instant you even made that decision about how your world is. What other meaning could you give to this event now? What learning and understanding could empower you for the future? How can you see that the meaning you gave it then does not need to colour your experience and outcomes anymore? The most effective way of changing a limiting decision like this is to work on the unconscious level, hence the NLP work, but you can do this consciously by yourself, it just may take a while longer because whatever you do, change occurs on the unconscious level. If you work directly with the unconscious it can shift quite quickly.

The other route is to work consciously, bring things in to your awareness so you can examine them and work on releasing them. You can start with a reality check – gather evidence to the contrary. Speak to your friends and family. Be honest with yourself about how much you have listened to that voice in the past and let it influence you. Explore new ways to prove the saboteur wrong. Take time to contemplate what comes up for you and know that you can choose to change this. Getting to the bottom of a belief is an insightful experience, like the time I realised that my father wasn't saying I was dumb. You will know when you've hit the jackpot – you get a certain feeling of ah-ha – that's it!

Once you unearth these kind of insights you can choose a different reality. Just because I didn't think I got my dream as a child does not mean that I cannot get my dream now. And it is a conscious choice. That's what living spiritually is about, we've said this before but I can't emphasise this enough. No one is going to come along and wave a magic wand to change your belief pattern, you have to a) want to change it, b) commit to change it and c) do it.

Each and every time you catch yourself thinking thoughts that stop you creating what you have decided you want, you need to consciously change your mind. Be disciplined, pray for the mental strength to have the will power to make these choices. Be present enough to make these choices. If you are working with abundance and catch yourself thinking or talking from a place of poverty consciousness, always focused on not having enough, immediately change the thought. It can be as subtle as changing the sentence, 'I can't afford it' which makes you feel a victim of your financial circumstances to 'I choose not to afford it today', the choice, once again, empowers you. As we said earlier; start to feel how it will be when you are wealthy, start acting from that feeling. Visualise it and each time you start to feel bad about money know that it is time to start changing your thoughts, replace the continuous tape that is playing in your head with the one that makes you feel good.

The impressions we carry round with us can sometimes come from previous lives. In fact, many of them are and we simply reinforce them in this lifetime. I'm sure that if I went to do some past life work I would find other occurrences that would reinforce my beliefs. It doesn't matter which lifetime you relate to, but it is important that you do find a situation that you can feel emotionally. One that you can physically feel the pain, sadness, anger, or whatever emotion it brought up in you at the time. If you can't feel the emotion then you are still analysing the situation in your mind and that is not the level that you need to work on. When you intellectualise things the ego can get involved and side-track you from resolving this issue and moving on. Once you access the emotional level you can start making the choices to move you forward from that belief.

To reinforce any work you do around beliefs, whether conscious or unconscious, start to put some new behaviours and boundaries in place to support yourself in the new, expanded place you now live from. What are three things you can do that pre-supposes the change you are embracing? For example, if you are working on changing the belief that you could never be the weight you want, start to take some extra exercise to reinforce your new belief that you can be your ideal weight. Drop one type of food that you know would make a difference.

These new behaviours need to be the kind of things you would do if you didn't believe that limiting decision you made many moons ago. Or maybe there are some boundaries you need to enforce. Telling your friends not to indulge your passion for ice cream when they invite you over for dinner would be one idea. All these new behaviours tell the unconscious mind that you have changed, shifted the beliefs you had, and you can now move forward, free from them once and for all.

The Power of Intention and Visualisation

Another useful tool in creating your reality is to use the power of intention and visualisation. When you work with these two aspects you are invoking the Law of Attraction. The DVD, *The Secret*, is an inspiration for using the Law of Attraction. It states that whatever you focus on you create. The movie was originally based on *The Teachings of Abraham with Esther and Jerry Hicks*. Abraham teaches that the Law of Attraction is a Universal Law, whether you are aware of it or not. What you think about and what you feel about, you bring about, thoughts become things. In the beginning of this chapter we talked about how everything originates from a single energetic Source. The power of attraction links back into that source. Time and time again I have seen with my clients how, when they get absolutely clear about some aspect of their life and create an intention, seeming miracles begin to happen. Add to that the power of visualisation and you get the Universe working in your favour.

A client of mine had moved her business into a good position, she had regular clients and was now earning enough to cover her expenses. It was time to move up a notch. She concentrated on defining her client profile. She became very clear on the type of clients she wanted, the size of the contract, the location of the clients, and the average amount of money she would earn. At the time she didn't know the 'how' but simply the 'what'. She then created a visualisation of how her life and business would feel once she had moved her business into this new paradigm. Every day she sat down for ten minutes undisturbed and ran through her visualisation, not just seeing what was happening, but also allowing herself to feel just how good it will feel once it has happened. She invoked her positive emotions and fuelled her visualisation with them. By focusing on this new intention her business began to move in the direction she wanted. Adverts that in the past had not brought any enquiries began to work for her. People who in the past didn't take up her quotations came back. She was introduced to contacts out of the blue who opened new doorways for her. Within two months she had moved the focus of her business. Now that's not to say she didn't put an effort into her business too – she did, she took action, and what she also did was hold fast to the intention, trust the visualisation, and, even more importantly, had fun with it. In the past she had wanted this level of business but always felt it unobtainable. She didn't know where to start. By defining exactly what she wanted, she brought an energetic support that is far greater then simple effort alone.

As we said earlier, when you create what you want in your life you have one very important support. Your emotions. Your emotions are your inner guidance system, they tell you when you are thinking something that is not in line with what you want to manifest. To create anything, you need to be thinking the right thoughts. It is impossible to monitor every thought you have. As we have explored earlier in the chapter we have some beliefs that do not fit with what we want, often these are limiting decisions and we are not even aware of thinking them. They will, however, make us feel a bit 'off'. Have you ever had a day when you just didn't feel happy but didn't know why? Chances are some unconscious thought was playing in the background. The unhappy feeling is a signal for you to pay attention. It is saying, 'hey, you're thinking something counter to your desires, listen up, change the thought'. At this moment you have a point of choice, you can choose to focus your attention somewhere else. This is very important, as the final stage in the creation process is receiving. You've asked, believed it to be true and now you need to receive. This is where the emotions come in. To receive, you have to keep the channel open, you need to hold the visualisation, fuel the positive belief and stay constant in your knowing. So often we start towards something we dream of, and just because it does not arrive as and when we thought it would, we quit, we give up. How many times has the Universe just been about to deliver to you something spectacular, but you've found some limit to stop you going on and the Universe has had to sigh, turn around and put it back in the cupboard again? Instead we need to stay steadfast, keep uppermost the feelings of joy, happiness, excitement and do all that we can to have our positive thoughts rule our minds. These are the components to manifestation, the bringing about of what we wish for. The Law of Attraction says like attracts like; to be a conscious part of the creative process our responsibility is to create the biggest and best magnet possible.

This three-fold process is truly taking responsibility for your life. You are part of the creative process; this clear message you send to the Universe can only be answered, never ignored. Some people complain that they do send messages but nothing ever materialises. When I explore this with them it often turns out that they are always changing their minds, never settling on one thing. How can a collection of contradictory messages be fulfilled? We need to be very clear on our intention and allow time for the Universe to work out a way to send us what we ask for, and even allow that we might be sent something even greater. We need to be flexible enough to see that sometimes the Universe will fill the order in a different way.

Why might our order be filled in a different way? If you step back to the bigger picture of life, that our life is the Earth School in which we learn to come back to ourselves, sometimes it is not in your best interests that you have this experience right now. What will be in your highest interest is that you have confronted and dealt with a limiting belief and that is what will bear fruit. You may think that you are doing this for one reason when in fact it may be for something much greater.

So often we put such small limits on our reality. This is where trust comes. You have to know that God will only give you the highest. Your part of the deal is to let go of the limits that hold you down in this world. To drop the 'how'. Your job is to work out what you want to have happen, the final result, be really clear on the outcome and what it will give you rather than the method. Sometimes you have no idea what's in store, you may be creating the Fiat Panda when God has the Rolls Royce in mind.

A lot of people would love to win the lottery, who wouldn't? A client of mine was starting up her own business and it was very tight financially. A large contract with a whole stack of money would have solved the problem there and then. One day we were talking and I asked her what she had learnt by being in such a tight situation. She told me that she had had to face her fears about being self-employed, about being able to deliver her service professionally, about being able to handle the big jobs. Each time she thought she had cracked it, another challenge would come her way and she would have to face yet more crippling beliefs and change them. When success finally came she could see that had she been bailed out by an early chunk of money she would never have faced her demons, and grown as a person and as a business women. All the struggles along the way were the gift in the situation and her Rolls Royce was the confidence that she had accrued along the way that now made her such a success.

Each challenge sent our way is exactly what we need in the moment, we are never sent a challenge too big for us, nor too small. Know that your side of the equation is to put in the self-effort, create the intention, work with the visualisation, feel the emotions of it being done and drop the limiting decisions. Then, and only then, once you no longer need or want anything on an egoic level, from a place of fear or scarcity, can things come to you. Living life at this level is a dichotomy so live it, play the game, work at creating the highest you can imagine, and always keep in mind that it is God's play, God's game. In this way you keep your sense of humour and you Remember Perfection.

Tips

- Become conscious of the power of your mind. Check in regularly where your mind is. Is it present? What fantasies is it creating right now? Are you even aware of the stories it is telling you? Use your emotions as your inner guidance, how you are feeling is indicative of what you are thinking. Only when you are present can you be a creative force.

- To dis-empower your limiting beliefs do the following exercise. It is best to do this over a few days as more beliefs will surface once you start the process. Take a sheet of paper and divide the page in two. On one side list all your beliefs. Once you have the full list, write next to each belief whose it is, where you learnt it; mother's, father's, teacher's, sibling's, priest's. Now take another look, is it really your belief? Is this truly your experience? Do you still wish to believe this, to live from this belief? If not, start the work to eradicate it from your operating system.

- Once you have become totally clear on what you want to create, set a specific intention. Remind yourself daily of your intention Take some time to visualise your intention. Play the scenario out in your mind, actually feel how excited you are as you see yourself being/doing/having. Energetically create a new paradigm.

- Believe that it is possible and know that once you have asked and believed it to be true that all you need to do is receive. To receive you need to be in that emotionally receptive space, so do all you can to stay in that positive mind space. Stay happy!

- To work on unearthing and resolving a belief you need to tap into the emotion behind it. You can start to release it once you can physically feel the pain, sadness, anger, or whatever emotion it brought up in you at the time. If you can't feel the emotion then you are still analysing the situation in your mind. Once you access the emotional level you can start making the choices to move you forward away from that belief.

- Become very clear as to what you want to create. Then stick to it. If you keep changing the request, sending contradictory messages you end up with no movement at all.

- When your wish is not fulfilled remember it may be because there is something in your highest interest happening. Trust the process, learn the lessons.

Contemplation

Give yourself at least half an hour for this contemplation. If you have a place within your home where you meditate use this space or if not just find somewhere quiet where you will not be disturbed. Have your journal or a notebook handy.

Before you start this contemplation identify one idea or phrase that stood out for you in this chapter. For example it might be about limiting beliefs. You now need to devise a question for you to contemplate. For example it could be 'what limiting beliefs stop me from living life fully?' Or 'what fears are behind my limiting beliefs?' Settle on whatever question feels right for you, something that will give you insight.

Get into a comfortable position and gently relax your body by taking some deep breaths. Breathe into any area of your body that holds tension and as you breathe out feel that tension flow out with your breath. Once you feel relaxed bring your breathing back to your normal rhythm and simply focus on your breath for a few minutes. At this point invite Grace into your contemplation in whatever way seems appropriate for you. Now ask yourself the question you wish to contemplate. Ask it three times and then simply sit and see what comes to mind. If you find your mind wandering simply bring it back to the question. After sitting with the question for a while pick up your pen and begin to write. Let the answer flow, do not censor it, stop it or word-craft it. Simply allow your wisdom to emerge. Once you have finished sit quietly for a moment and acknowledge the wisdom and insight received.

CHAPTER FIVE

Reality and Attitude

Atttitude is the key to our reality.

There is another side to creating your reality and that is free will. We have a destiny to fulfil in this and every lifetime. Karma comes back into the picture once again. I believe that I have a certain set of experiences to work with in this lifetime. They are created by the set of beliefs I bring with me into this life and the karma that I am to experience. When these experiences happen in my life I can create my reality in how I deal with what is happening.

How can I do that? How can I create my reality when something happens *to* me? How do I stop myself feeling a victim of the world? If I lose my job how can I create a reality about that? I've lost my job, period. No. The experience (karma) is that I have lost my job. That is a true situation in the physical realm. My reality, however, comes from what I make of that experience. I can choose my attitude to the external play that goes on around me. I can choose what is real in this moment. I can find an alternative way of looking at and seeing a situation that will give me an opposite experience. So often in our western society we choose to play the victim, to blame someone else, as if the idea of being responsible for our experience of our lives does not even compute. In truth not only are we 100% responsible for our response to our lives but we are also responsible for everything that happens in our lives.

Some people have a problem with this statement and pull out lots of examples of how this simply cannot be true. But think on this, if you choose to believe this statement is true and then live accordingly just think how different your life would be.

Our minds are very powerful. You can let this power run without control and buy into the blame culture or you can harness this power to your own advantage. You can choose what your mind will focus on – the 'poor me' or the opportunity. The choice is yours. The great philosopher Kahlil Gibran wrote in his poem, *The Prophet,* 'Your pain is the breaking of the shell that encloses your understanding.' He went on to say, 'Much of your pain is self-chosen. It is the bitter potion by which the physician within you heals your sick self.' Our higher self, the God within, knows what is best for our Soul. What we may judge as pain, unfairness, bad luck, is most likely to be exactly what we need to grow. As Gibran goes on to say, 'Therefore trust the physician, and drink his remedy in silence and tranquillity.' In other words choose your attitude to what is happening, choose not to make it personal and wrong, but rather see the perfection.

A client I was working with experienced how the power of the mind not only created her reality, but also how she could choose a different one. She was unable to work and her husband was self-employed, but his business was not doing very well. He went for a meeting with a company to talk about a freelance contract that would turn their fortunes around. After the first interview he was told that it was virtually certain that the contract was his. He just had to meet with the other partners and finalise finances. With this in mind they went off to visit her sister for a holiday feeling very abundant. They had a great week, no worries for the first time in a long while, good company, fun times. In their minds everything was sorted.

On the way back from the holiday he called the company to arrange the second meeting only to find that they had given someone else the contract. She was devastated, suddenly everything crumbled away and she could only see lack. She felt that the whole world was conspiring against her, so much so that when she went out for breakfast and opened a butter pack which had melted, and it poured all over her, she became distraught. It was the straw that broke the camel's back, the final proof that life was against her. All the bottled-up emotion and fear came tumbling out. On her return, we talked about it, I asked her, "What's changed? How is your actual situation different from when we talked two weeks ago?" Her husband had never had the job, the money, the security – it had all been in her mind. In her mind she had created all these things and now, in her mind, she had lost them. The truth of the matter was that nothing had changed. Although tough, it was a great realisation for her and showed how powerful the mind is.

She could choose to see it as an experience, a lesson, rather than a tragedy of huge proportion. She could choose her attitude to what had happened rather than feel a victim of circumstance. A postscript to this story is that a couple of months later a much better opportunity came along and things did improve. Just not to their schedule or in the way they had thought it would. In fact, better.

This is the free will element we have in our lives. We have the free will to choose our attitude to any situation that occurs in our life. Byron Katie, in her book, *Loving What Is,* challenges us to question the reality we have created in our minds. The full-blown scenarios that we watch unfold, get attached to and then think are real. By asking ourselves, 'who would we be without that thought?', without that scenario playing in our mind, we put the element of choice back into our lives. This clever question shows us immediately that we can choose our reality. By shining a light on the thought we can choose not to think it. Then, by looking for one stress-free reason to hold onto that thought, we begin to see when we are reluctant to drop a thought. I have never found a stress-free reason to hold onto a thought that creates a negative reality. Certainly, we can come up with many reasons not to drop a thought but never a stress-free reason. Once we can make that level, conscious choice rather than be at the mercy of our fickle mind and its fears then life does become far more fun.

Being Present in our Reality

We are so used to living in the mind. We create whole lifetimes in our fantasies, some great, some scary, depending on how positive or negative our mental state is at the time. The key to noticing the moment of choice, which reality will we live in, is being present. Living with awareness. We can only notice what tricks the mind is getting up to if we are present, in the moment. When we are present, the mind can only focus on what is. It cannot worry about the future and create possible futures for us to get obsessed with. Nor can it relive the past and create all those 'if onlys'. Being present is the only way you can create your reality. If you are truly present then you can choose what to experience in that moment.

It is our past and our attachment to it that keeps us from being present. Each event that we still have an energetic charge for holds us back from being totally here. We are energetic beings and there is a constant flow of universal energy through us and around us. These energy circuits relate to specific chakras within our body. A chakra, in the Indian mystic tradition, is an energy centre within our subtle body that relates not only to our physical well-being but to our emotional and spiritual well-being too. These energy circuits relate to all areas of our lives, for example creativity, vitality, intellect, will, survival, personal power, emotions, choice. To be fully present we need all our energy to be in present time. If we are still resentful about a situation that happened twenty years ago, something sarcastic a sibling said to us for example, our energy relating to that area of our body and psyche is not in present time. It is still feeding an event from twenty years ago.

To get ourselves into present time we need to identify every stream of energy that is not here and pull it back. A good exercise each morning before you get out of bed is to ask yourself, 'where is my energy flowing?' This may be a physical sensation or simply something that you notice your mind is on. Each and every time you notice this, visualise pulling that cord of energy back into yourself. You can even say something like, 'I simply don't have time for you today, I choose not to give you energy'.

Another practice for being in the present moment is to live a daily awareness of being part of everything – practise being the witness of your world. In Tibetan Buddhism they have fifty-nine slogans called the *lojong* teachings that remind us how to awaken our hearts. One of them is, 'Of the two witnesses, hold the principal one.' By this it means there are two types of witnesses in our lives, all those people outside of us who have an opinion about everything we do, and ourselves. We are the principal witness of ourselves. Focus on the principal one. If you have problems being your own witness then just pretend, act as if, and get into it that way. Put yourself in the picture. If you're walking down a street with two friends, change your awareness to there being three people walking down the street – count yourself in. This subtle shift puts you in the picture and removes any level of separation – you're no longer separate from your life, you're part of your life and you are present in your life.

When I want to count myself in I look out of the window at the wonderful view. There below me is the sea with its white horses dancing on the tops of the waves, the brilliant sun in the blue sky, the old white Andalucian town to my right, its castle guarding the town. I then add myself to the picture. I see myself sitting here on the third floor looking at this scene below. I ask myself who is the seer, who is looking out of my eyes? This brings me to the present. It makes it real.

One way to help us witness our thoughts is through a regular practise of meditation. Meditation, contrary to common belief, isn't a stopping of all thought, although that can be an experience of meditation, but it is rather a witnessing of all thought. One of the simplest versions of meditation is to watch your breath. Simply focus on the breath as it comes in and goes out. Thoughts will continue as it is the mind's function to think and doubt. At some point you will realise that you are 'thinking' a thought. You have caught the thought and run with it. At this point, simply label the thought 'thinking' and go back to the breath. If you do this or any other type of meditation regularly you will find that you will begin to catch your thoughts more easily. You will become the witness of your thoughts rather than be caught up in the dramas as they unfold in your mind.

You can use the principle of meditation at any time of the day not just in your formal practise. By simply stopping and becoming conscious of the breath and your thoughts you become present. Once we have trained ourselves to become the witness as much as possible our lives can become more engaging. When we become more present, more in the moment, we see how we are creating through our thoughts. By being present we choose our attitude moment to moment because, for the first time ever, we are able to witness our thoughts, and therefore, consciously change them if we want.

I became very conscious of the power of my own mind as I was walking in the ashram grounds one day. This was about nine years ago and I cannot remember for the life of me what I was thinking about. I do recall, however, the incredibly distressed state I was in. I wasn't crying; I was distraught. Something that hadn't occurred, was unlikely to occur and was simply in my mind had created this reaction. At one point a voice in my head said, 'this isn't real'. Immediately I saw how ridiculous my distress was. I was in a terrible state over something my mind had concocted. I started to laugh. The fantasy disappeared like a bubble popping. This strong experience has stayed with me ever since, even though I can't remember what it was that upset me so much. Each time my mind starts to create nightmare fantasies, I remember it and it brings me back to reality.

As we stop being run by our subconscious beliefs, limiting decisions and the fantasies of our mind we can start to consciously create our world. This is the true benefit of being present and creating reality. When we see that we have choice, that we are not ruled by the world around us, but rather, are able to choose our world both within and around us, life becomes vibrant and exciting. Our thinking then immediately reflects in how we perceive the world personally. We begin to work in collaboration with God. Co-creating our world. You are part of the process of creation, your thoughts, beliefs and attitudes count. Make them good ones.

The Relationship between Creating Reality and Fear

Our fears are a large part of creating our reality. As I have already mentioned we are very good at creating our negative beliefs, our fears. So what is fear, how does it manifest in our lives? Fear takes us out of the moment. Fear is totally in the mind. One definition I like is: fear is False Evidence Appearing Real. This false evidence arises in our minds. However, only by us buying into the fear can it feel real and influence our world. Once we explore our fears we begin to see how insidious they are. Fears have the quality of a shape-shifter, for they move and change depending on circumstance and our strength of mind and therefore, as such, can have a huge influence on our lives.

I acknowledge that some fears are useful. These are the fears that keep us safe. The feeling we get when we get too close to a sheer cliff is the fear that stops us going too close and falling over. These are the sensible fears and there is nothing wrong with them at all. I call these our instinctual fears. They are healthy and part of our necessary survival kit. It is the mental imagined fears that we need to face and move past.

> Instinctual fears are useful...

> OOPS! MAYBE I SHOULD HAVE LISTENED TO THAT ONE!

The reason I make a distinction between the two is that mentally imagined fear is totally self-created, and more often than not does not serve us well. This kind of fear is a reaction, governed by what is created in our minds, rather than a response that relates to what is true right now. These mental fears can be dispelled from our lives, or at least disempowered. We have all heard of times when people have acted fearlessly. For example, when a person puts their career in jeopardy by becoming the whistle blower in an unjust situation. Their belief in 'rightness', acting on what is true for them, focuses them into the present moment where fear cannot be present. 'It was just the right thing to do', 'I just did it' are often things they will say after the event. And it is true, that heartfelt response created the reality of no fear.

Some people live their lives ruled by one fear or another. Many of these fears are phobias created by some experience in the past or even in past lives. They are mostly irrational to everyone except the person who is held in their thrall. But, to that person they are paralysing. I have seen a friend go to pieces with the idea of flying in a plane. If it hadn't been so real for her it would have been funny. I took her up to the airport the night before her flight and she and I sat watching the planes take off and land at Heathrow airport. Maybe not the best thing for a flying phobic but she thought it might get her used to the idea; that and a few rum and cokes. Each time a plane took off she would say something like, "Oh my God it's going so slow, how can it possible fly, it will never get off the ground." The next minute a plane would land and she'd be off saying, "Oh my God it's going so fast it's going to hit the ground. Oh my God, it's so close to the ground!" However much I reassured her with the theory of aerodynamics all she could see was disaster – from all angles. The irony of this story is that she survived the flight really well and was feeling so pleased with herself that she got the hotel in Paris, waltzed into the lift (another phobia of hers) without thinking and promptly got stuck in it for three hours. It doesn't matter what you do, eventually you will manifest those fears, so start looking at them now.

We are what we think and we have the freedom to choose what we think – when we remember. Fear is very strong and often we are deep into a scenario in our minds before we realise what we are doing – if we do realise at all. What you resist persists, what you fear, what you constantly think about, is created. It is very important to look at our fears and face them. Ignoring them does not work, they are hooked deep inside of us and unless we bring them into the full light and find the root of the fear then it will carry on creating on some level of our life.

We are what we think.

OH NO !!!

Often fear seems irrational when brought out into the light. It may be based on an experience we had when we were young. It is possible that at the time the response from us was appropriate, what is scary to a five-year-old isn't necessarily to a thirty-five year old. However, it is possible to work with it and release the fear and replace it with an appropriate response. Others may be more deeply rooted and it may take more work, maybe with help, to release the grip that fear has on us. Whichever it is I recommend facing them and dealing with them.

We often do things motivated by fear. We will do something to stop something we fear from happening. The problem with this scenario is that if we do something out of fear, with the energy of fear, even though what we do might be good, we will still manifest the fear. A client of mine thought that she was about to lose a contract for some regular work she had been doing. It wasn't a huge part of her income, but every little helped so she really did not want to lose it and was fearful of the consequences should it happen. Because of this she decided that if she did some extra work it would stand out and make her look very efficient and on the ball, and then maybe they would decide that they couldn't do without her.

She lost the contract, and afterwards realised why. The main problem in her thinking was that she was doing the work from fear of loss. The energy she brought to the work was lack. By doing the work from fear she had merely ensured that she manifested it. Nothing done with fear as its sponsoring thought can benefit you. Look very closely at what you do from fear in your life. These fears will always hold a lesson for you. They will highlight something in you that you need to address in some way or another. Make a list of the fears that rule anything that you do. Ask yourself whether you truly wish to do these things anymore. There may be ones that you decide you do wish to keep on doing. If that is the case great but, and it is an important but, from this point forward do them with love. Offer your effort with love, offer the fruits of your effort with love and have no expectations as to what or how it benefits you.

For the ones you choose not to continue with, set yourself a plan and timeline for letting them go. This may include informing anyone who may be involved with this action so they know how you wish to be in the future. It might be identifying different aspects of what you fear and seeking solutions for each. One thing you can do is decide how you wish to act the next time you are confronted by the fear. In that way you have an alternative way of dealing with a situation already worked out. Envision yourself in a similar situation and feel how you would like to act in future. What might you say, how could you respond differently. Forewarned is forearmed in these situations. And it is a type of fight, a fight against an old way of being and a tapping into the courage within. In this way you will begin the process of ruling these fear-based actions from your life. This is another way to create your reality.

Often it seems that we almost have to manifest or get close to manifesting our fears before we can see them for what they are. One phrase I had in my head in the past was: 'I will never be a bag lady on the streets.' Now I used this phrase in many tight situations and I had always said it feeling reassured to know that I wouldn't be on the streets. Things may get bad but never that bad. What I didn't realise was behind that phrase was the actual huge fear of being on the streets. I had subconsciously thought that as long as I believed this phrase I would be 'safe'. One of the problems with this statement is that our unconscious mind doesn't register a negative, thus my mind was hearing 'I will be a bag lady'.

By saying this phrase to myself I was actually saying that the worst thing that could happen to me would be to be on the streets, to be homeless, no money, desolate. I have no idea where this fear comes from, not this lifetime surely, as I come from a safe, middle-class English family, so it hasn't been my experience this time round. Then again, maybe the fact that I have been protected from that experience in this lifetime created a fear about how I would survive such an experience. The possibilities are endless, and in truth it really doesn't matter how I came to fear it, what matters is that I saw it and dealt with it. However, sometimes our fears hide behind what we think are positive image beliefs. I had the image that being on the streets would not happen to me. I only saw this fear in its true colours when I sat down one day when I was in a tight spot and thought to myself, 'Oh my God, if I'm not careful I'll be on the streets.' It hit me at that moment how a huge fear had hidden so cleverly for so long.

Our ego often plants a fear so that we will not change. I saw that my fear of being on the streets had not always been with me. I realised when I contemplated it, that it had sneaked its way into my mind when I started to live life more fully. When I started to take risks, not conform to popular societal ways of doing things – when I committed to change. To stop, or at least slow down this progress, the ego planted a fear. Change means death to the ego and it fights back dirty. Before my commitment to allow change in my life this fear about being homeless had not been in my mind.

I encourage you to take a good look at that belief sheet you created in the previous chapter, or if you haven't done it yet then do it now. Fears and beliefs are tightly interwoven and it is useful to see fears you hold that are masquerading as beliefs. Another exercise is to write down all your fears. It is very useful to actually see all your fears on paper. And I mean all. The little silly ones you won't admit to anyone as well as the huge, breath-stopping ones. Write them all down, every one relating to every aspect of life. It may take a few days to catch them all, keep adding to the list if you need to. They may include being alone, poor, out of work, unloved, rejected, losing your health or being ostracised. Fears manifest in many different ways and what may be scary for one may be like water off a duck's back for another. When you've got your definitive list, take a look at each fear you've written and ask yourself, 'am I really run by this fear?' Three answers may come:

A) No, not any more.

B) No, and actually this was never truly my fear but one taught to me by others.

C) Yes.

Fear is often a habit and we think that we are still ruled by a particular fear when in fact it is one that we have conquered as in answer A. A client of mine saw that she used to have a fear about being judged by others for being fat. She hated being visible and rarely walked through the centre of a crowded room. As we discussed fears she realised that actually this did not rule her anymore, it was an old fear that she had gotten over, but she still had it in her list. As you review your list notice the ones that, although they may have been true in the past, no longer are – acknowledge this, and give yourself a pat on the back and take them off the list of fears forever.

Answer B may surprise you too. Quite often we own a fear that is not ours. It may be something you picked up in your family as a child or something you heard and took on board without consciously evaluating it for yourself. Now, when you come to look at it in the light of day, you see that in fact it is not something that you fear at all, you can handle it no problem. The mother of a friend of mine had a fear of going into a shop and not buying something. She felt so self-conscious that each time she entered a shop she would buy an item even if she didn't want anything. My friend used to feel the same way until she realised that in fact this was not her 'stuff' at all, but her mother's. Once she realised, she began to practise only browsing and it became fun. She no longer had to buy. So, if you identify any of these types of fear, the ones that are not truly yours, cross them off your list too, and acknowledge yourself as well.

So, you are now left with the C answers. Those that still have hold over you. Now is the time to start addressing those fears. You can either do this alone, meditating on them, delving into the root of them as you did with beliefs and seeing them for what they are – False Evidence Appearing Real. Or if this seems too difficult on your own and you feel it would help, work with a counsellor who can help you explore your fears and learn to release them. Fear can be worked on in many ways, seeing it for what it is and understanding why we have a fear can begin the process. Again, NLP is very useful for addressing fears as you can go back in your unconscious to the first (it is the first event that is important here) event when fear took root and learn something different from that experience which in turn releases the fear.

One useful exercise to break the grip of a fear is to play 'make it worse'. Ask yourself how this could be worse. There are two ways you can approach your answer. Firstly, dis-empower the fear by blowing it up so large that it explodes like a balloon. Keep on asking yourself 'how could this get worse' until it builds to such a ridiculous size, with fantasy outcomes that it becomes too big for you to take seriously. For example, someone I know gets fearful when she has to present her work. She knows it is good and has always had good feedback. Still she gets fearful at each new presentation. By blowing the scenario up in her mind and seeing people laugh at her work, making snidy comments and generally deriding her efforts she herself can see how silly her fear is. Deep down she knows she is good and that's what makes it through when she faces the fear, it is another way of getting real.

When you do this you begin to see the power of your mind and how it hi-jacks your confidence. You can then choose to think differently and this is where the second approach comes in. Go back to your first answer of the question 'what could be worse?' Take a look at the answer before it got to a silly size and ask yourself what you would do if faced with that scenario. In this way your mind starts to create solutions to deal with whatever may happen. This in turn helps you see that you are not power-less in the face of experience, rather you can see the steps and have the tools to take the necessary action. In the face of this knowledge fear dissipates.

Only by shining this depth of light on fear can you start to see that it has no truth in your life. Our basic fear and the root of all fears is that of personal, physical survival, it takes many forms and needs close examining. This is one of the reasons for our spiritual search, why we strive to apply the spiritual principles in our daily lives. Once we have the experience that we are not separate from life, from God, then our fear loosens its grip until we get to the place that fear has no hold at all. At this point creating our reality rises to another level, we begin to believe that anything is possible and start to aim for the highest goals. Life becomes truly inspired and inspirational.

You can learn to step into a world free from the bondage of fear. Boundaries previously inhibiting us from creating the life we want dissolve. As each fear is seen for what it is, and released, we step into a place of power. Power to create our reality. We move one step nearer to the time when we can respond rather than react to a situation. We use our free will to shape our attitude, define our choices, take responsibility for our world. We become empowered. Empowered to work with the God within and responsibly create a fearless world.

And move one more step towards Remembering Perfection.

Tips

- When you feel the victim of circumstance or that you have no control over what is happening, remember the one thing you always can choose is your attitude. By choosing your attitude to what is happening, you can create a new reality.

- Be present, it is the only place in which you can create reality. Count yourself in the picture. Once a day stop what you are doing and add yourself into the picture of your life, it could be while you are brushing your teeth or having a shower in the morning. The more often you do this the more likely you will remember throughout the day.

- If you are not a regular meditator, start a practise of regular meditation. Learn to watch your thoughts. It will help throughout your day, not only through catching your thoughts and choosing your personal reality – your attitude, but bringing a level of calmness to your whole being in the world.

- Watch for fears hiding behind positive belief statements. When you catch them, work with the fear. This will change the energy behind the statement and empower its truth.

- As you begin to unearth your fears, write them down and see whose they are. When you identify those that still have a hold in your life, work with them to loosen their grip in your life. You can live without them.

- Play 'make it worse' with your fears. Dis-empower them and then see how, if you examine them and their possible consequences, you can handle whatever comes your way.

- Let love motivate your actions. Any action motivated by fear will only create the fear.

Contemplation

Give yourself at least half an hour for this contemplation. If you have a place within your home where you meditate use this space, or if not just find somewhere quiet where you will not be disturbed. Have your journal or a notebook handy.

Before you start this contemplation identify one idea or phrase that stood out for you in this chapter. For example, it might be the idea that you can choose not to be a victim. You now need to devise a question for you to contemplate. It could be, 'in what ways do I allow myself to be a victim?' Or, 'what would choosing to take responsibility look like for me?' Settle on whatever question feels right for you, something that will give you insight into the idea.

Get into a comfortable position and gently relax your body by taking some deep breaths. Breathe into any area of your body that holds tension and as you breathe out feel the tension flowing out with your breath. Once you feel relaxed bring your breathing back to your normal rhythm and simply focus on your breath for a few minutes. At this point invite Grace into your contemplation in whatever way seems appropriate for you. Now ask yourself the question you wish to contemplate. Ask it three times and then simply sit and see what comes to mind. If you find your mind wandering, simply bring it back to the question and listen for the answer. When you feel moved pick up your pen and begin to write. Let the words flow, do not censor or word-craft it. Simply allow your wisdom to emerge. Once you have finished sit quietly for a moment and acknowledge the wisdom and insight received.

CHAPTER SIX

Unconditional Love

*Love is our true essence
– the answer to the question, 'Who am I?'*

We've looked at some of the ways we can live our lives spiritually but what more will help us? What alchemical ingredient do we need to add to the mix, to make it all the more potent? How about love? Love, that misunderstood, misused word that is at the centre of our world, both physically, emotionally, and metaphysically.

What is love? It can be lots of things to many people. However, I'm not talking about the 'greeting card' version of love, the sugary, romantic love that we see in the movies. I'm talking unconditional love. Not the token love that is measured by what we do but rather a love that values what we are. For example, your partner can give you a gift out of guilt (greeting card version) or out of pure appreciation for who you are (unconditional). The gift is the same but the energy behind this gift defines its true value. Love is our essence, it is who we are in our purest sense.

When we live love, we live in divinity.

In this chapter we will explore this love. What does it look like within our relationships? We will discover how we can cultivate an awareness of unconditional love through how we relate to ourselves. We will delve into the idea of unconditionality and how it can help us in our everyday life.

What is Unconditional Love?

Unconditional love asks for nothing in return. Our minds and ego often fight this version of love. We can think of many reasons why it is not possible. It is simply too challenging for some people. Common retorts to the idea of unconditional love are: 'there's no such thing as unconditional love'; 'that's fine but what's in it for me?', 'love is a two-way currency' 'that's all well and good but I need to be needed'. These statements show the struggle we have with the idea even though in our heart of hearts we may embrace it.

Unless you were extraordinarily luckyYou were probably not always shown the model of unconditional love within your family in your childhood. This is not a criticism of your family – even the most loving ones have conditions at some time or another. Often, even though we may have known that our parents loved us totally, they still may not have been strong enough to live this love all the time. Stress, tiredness, frustration and simply getting through life can get in the way of being unconditional. There are, however, times when we have witnessed and sometimes experienced examples of unconditional love. Those pure moments of love between parent and child or the moment you truly wish for a friend to succeed no matter how it might impact you. Sadly though, love so often has conditions hanging off it even if they are never voiced or intended.

A poignant story about a four-year-old boy illustrates this perfectly. Martin was sitting with his grandmother one day as she read him a story. Sitting at her feet, he was the perfect picture of innocence and love. Looking at him, her heart swelled and out of the blue she murmured, "Oh Martin, I do love you!"

He looked up at her and the immediate four-year-old answer was "…but?"

Within our culture our children pick up on the idea of conditional love. The conditions of: "I do love you… but I wish you would…"

If this is such an ingrained part of our world why change it? Why aim for unconditional love in the first place? If that's how our world works then what's to change? Nothing, if you are truly happy with it. However, I have yet to meet someone who expresses a desire to live life spiritually that is happy with the conditions placed on love. In our old conditional view of the world love is something given, bought, bargained for, traded. We do things out of fear of losing love. Love is used as a bribe. How often in relationships are the words 'I would love you if you would just…' uttered?

Love is the secret sensation of the Self.

I LOVE ME!

Are you tired of the old bartering for love? Does your heart yearn for a different experience of love? Have you started to see that love is actually not something that anyone can give you but rather something that resides inside you? A great saint once said, "Love is the secret sensation of the Self". I love this as it helps me get a feeling of the love that is us. That idea of a secret sensation somehow makes it tangible. Just close your eyes and repeat the sentence, what does it make you feel? Love is you, an experience that no other can give you. Once you radiate love you can then share the experience of it with others who then, in turn, find it within themselves. Unconditional love can be seen to be a contagious virus that can spread like wildfire around the world.

Imagine this – a growing number of people in the world who come from unconditional love to the best of their abilities. What would their and your life look like? I think that people would be less angry and frustrated with their world. They would smile more and notice the good more than the bad. Their support for each other would be unconditional. No longer would people hold back in fear of losing something if another succeeded. As a community we would take total responsibility of our lives and our choices. Blame would be a thing of the past. We would live in the present moment instead of worrying about our future or regretting our past.

Unconditional love is the hardest type of love and the most rewarding. It expects nothing. It simply is, just for love's sake. Unconditional love looks like it gives you nothing, but in truth it gives you back to yourself.

Love is our nascent state. We do not have to go anywhere, do anything or be with anyone to get love, to experience love. We already are love. This love permeates all actions of the Self, for love is the Self. Unconditional love has no price tag so in effect you give this love without attachment, desire, expectation or addiction. In this space is a great freedom, for if we give love like this then we stop being bound by our fears. By living unconditional love you become love, you become who you already are. Note I said 'living' – it is not that you can even give or take this love – you can only be it.

WE NEED TO LOVE OURSELVES BEFORE WE CAN LOVE OTHERS.

Unconditional Love in Relationships

I practise living this love to the best of my ability in my relationship. In our early days I used to play out the conditioning belief that in a relationship you do what pleases your partner. Whether this pleased me I didn't take into consideration. You can look at this 'pleasing other' from many levels. If we truly believe that we are all one, that there is only unity and that our feeling of separation is purely an illusion, then the highest understanding would be that there is no 'other'. From this understanding there is no need to try to please another in detriment to myself. However, as much as we might intellectually understand this viewpoint, it is not our everyday experience. When I feel separate, this view of non-duality, although totally true, sometimes doesn't always help the nitty-gritty situations I find myself in.

By playing the pleasing game in my relationship I was not living love. I was trying to control while looking loving. I also felt very hard done by at the same time. For example, whenever I was given the choice of where to go out for dinner I would always play the 'I don't mind – whatever you want' game. When in truth my poor, long-suffering partner wanted me to make a decision. Any decision. I then would silently feel hard done by because we hadn't gone where I wanted to go. This consistent pleasing 'other' is a subtle way of not taking responsibility within a relationship, a way of being a victim too.

It is also very annoying. I kept being told to please myself but I somehow couldn't hear that; it went totally against my beliefs. I became a doormat with a 'walk all over me' mentality. Now I don't live with a monster, but if you say enough times to someone 'walk all over me' then eventually they will. They will make all the decisions and get on with their life. This then led me into feeling very sorry for myself. Whenever I didn't voice a preference I would also feel hard done by because I couldn't understand why this didn't please. It was a no-win vicious circle.

As luck (God?) would have it I was invited to a seminar illustrating how spiritual practises aid us in our life. Part of the preparation was to contemplate and create a talk using a situation in my life as the subject matter. As I was dealing with my own personal relationship issues at the time I chose unconditional love within relationships. As I contemplated and wrote about it I began to see how tricky my ego is. Worse, this was not even a conscious choice. I began to see that my version of unconditional love was the most conditional love possible. My adaptation was 'you can do whatever you want as long as you promise to never leave me'. How big a condition is that? 'Why' I hear you cry 'of course you'd say that, you're in a relationship, that's part of the deal.'

No it is not. This is the largest condition of all. It is also an insidious version of conditional love in that it is unspoken. It rules all decisions and makes the relationship very dependent but it is never seen for what it is. Once you see this scenario playing out it helps to set the scene for real unconditional love to flourish. From that experience I wrote what I truly felt that unconditional love is between two people. A reminder for us all when we get into the blame mentality. Something to come back to and touch base with when we forget.

A love of the Soul saying:

> *'I will love you whatever you do as an expression of who you are in this moment. I see you, I am you and whatever you do in your life is your decision. If you choose to live your life with me that's great. If you choose to do something that challenges me I will deal with this and not try to change you. I will make my own choices in light of yours, but not governed by yours. I do not promise to*

like everything you do but I do promise to support your highest growth and equally I will make choices to support mine. I will take responsibility both for my life and love in my life. I will share this experience of love with you.'

This type of love challenges many people, as our society does not teach us of unconditional love. If you live this type of love, none of the 'payment' systems of our cultural system will work – you cannot tie needs to it. You cannot use love to be the rescuer; you cannot be the victim of love; you cannot be the prostitute for love – either in the traditional sense or in the sense of staying in a relationship because of financial security. Nor can you be the businessman/woman for love, negotiating deals of how love is equal for both – I'll give you this if you'll give me that. None of these old ways of being will work anymore.

True unconditional love has no rules, no contracts, no agreements and no payoffs. True unconditional love is totally free; it costs nothing to give and nothing to receive. It is limited to no one. You can love as many people as you want; you can feel that deep-heart connection with one or a hundred people. The choice is yours.

This, of course, brings up the question of fidelity and jealousy. So often we are brought up to think that we can only love one person, one special person, that Soul mate. If we love more than one we are unfaithful and it threatens our primary relationship. I believe these are two completely different and separate situations.

I love my partner, deeply and as unconditionally as I can from moment to moment. That doesn't mean that we don't drive each other nuts every now and again. I just love to the best of my ability. I also love many other people. Friends who I have known for years, people I meet for the first time and love instantly, those who I have known for lifetimes. I choose only one as my partner. I choose to give exclusivity – not of my love but of my person, my focus, my commitment, my support, my desire to share of myself at a deep level, one to one. This is a constantly renewing choice. I cannot say I promise to be with you for the rest of my life but I can and do say that at this moment in time I would like to be with you for the rest of my life.

By making this level of commitment and constantly renewing it then the love between two people is always fresh, new and never taken for granted. This love also demands very clear, honest communication. It means that you cannot blithely say 'I love you' when actually something else is going on. It means that sometimes you are going to say something that may not be what the other person wants to hear. It means that you may be in a space that you cannot truly say you feel that love right now. In these times know one thing – that love is always present. We do not lose love it is just that sometimes something shields that love from you so you cannot see or feel it. Sometimes these shields are emotional upheavals. Other times they are when fear gets a grip of us. The love still exists behind these shields, our task is to identify the shield and do whatever is necessary to remove it. When you do this, love will flow through your life again.

- THAT'S WHEN YOU INTERRUPTED ME.
- THAT'S WHEN I FELT STUPID IN FRONT OF YOUR MOTHER.
- THAT'S WHEN I THOUGHT YOU WERE ANGRY WITH ME.

Identify the shields.

If you feel this happening in your life, if you cannot find the love behind the shield, stop and take a step back. Take time to reconnect to your heart where love resides. One way to reconnect to your heart is to do a meditation on the heart, and to help you there is a suggested meditation in the tips section at the end of this chapter. Become clear as to what is blocking you from feeling that love right now. Is it anger, fear, resentment, jealousy, pride? Once you have identified it, you can then make choices to deal with it and remove it. Take responsibility for the love in your life, it is not something outside of you but within, it is up to you to find it.

When I saw the game of conditional love I had been playing I recognised immediately the truth of unconditional love – being love. It was as if a screen had been removed and I experienced that 'ah-ha' moment of truth. Alas, I don't live there permanently – not by a long shot – but I have had a glimpse of what it means and it carries great beauty. It is the end goal of the journey of our life and there are many things that we can do to help us move towards it.

From time to time I encourage you to take an honest look at the quality of the love within your relationships, be they with your partner or your friends and family. It is always useful to review the love in your life and whether it has become conditional. Are you adding conditions in fear of losing love? Have you lost sight of the fact that the love is inside you and that all you can do is to share that love? How open are you to love? How much do you allow people in? All these questions will bring you closer to your heart and therefore to love.

When we run our lives by conditions, e.g. the 'I will love you if you promise to only spend time with me' or the 'If you loved me you would lose weight' all we really succeed in doing is cause stress and pain. We put an intense pressure on those we supposedly love and create impossible expectations. In our minds things happen that we think shouldn't be happening. People don't live up to our expectations and as a consequence we often feel unheard and unloved. This makes us think that life is unfair.

However, if we begin to love those around us and ourselves unconditionally, from a place of 'not needing anything to change for us to feel love', we begin to Remember Perfection.

Tips

- If you cannot find the love behind the shield, stop and take a step back. Reconnect with your heart using the meditation below. Become clear as to what is blocking you from feeling that love right now. Is it anger, fear, resentment, jealousy, pride? Once you have identified it, make choices to deal with it and remove it, more often than not this includes honest communication. Again you may find you would like to work with someone to help you do this.

- Meditation on the heart.
  Find a quiet time, probably better in the morning so your mind is not racing with the day's thoughts. Sit in a comfortable, upright posture and take some deep breaths and become aware of your body. Now focus on your heart area, this is where your energetic heart centre lies. Breathe deeply into your heart and with each breath gradually feel yourself moving down into your heart. As you enter your heart take a look around, what do you see? What do you feel whilst resting in your heart? Reconnect with any feelings that are there. What is blocking the feeling of love in your heart? Recognise that these feelings are just energy and as such can be released. Breathe into these feelings and with each out-breath see them flowing out of your heart and see love flowing back in. Stay in your heart for as long as you wish, and when you feel you are ready, you can bring your awareness back to the room, bringing with you the feeling of love. As you take some deep breaths wiggle your toes to begin to feel your body and when you are ready open your

eyes. Know that this love you have just connected with is your love, it is the essence of you and you can access it at any time you wish.

- Copy the reminder about unconditional love, put it somewhere that you will see it, have it in your agenda, by your bed. Let it sink into your being. Or better still write your own!

The Love Of The Soul

'I will love you whatever you do as an expression of who you are in this moment. I see you, I am you and whatever you do in your life is ok. If you choose to live your life with me that's great. If you choose to do something that challenges me I will deal with this and not try to change you. I will make my own choices in light of yours, but not governed by yours. I do not promise to like everything you do but I do promise to support your highest growth and equally I will make choices to support mine. . I will take responsibility both for my life and love in my life. I will share this experience of love with you.'

- Every now and again take an honest look at the quality of the love within your relationships, be they with your partner or your friends and family. How conditional are they? Where can you let go of conditions? Make sure you talk about your insights with the person involved.

- When you catch yourself holding love back, putting a condition in it, ask yourself – what am I frightened of? What would happen if I loved unconditionally right now? Each small step brings you into a greater experience of love.

Contemplation

Give yourself at least half an hour for this contemplation. If you have a place within your home where you meditate use this space or if not just find somewhere quiet where you will not be disturbed. Have your journal or a notebook handy.

Before you start this contemplation identify one idea or phrase that stood out for you in this chapter. For example, it might be the idea of taking responsibility for love in your life. You now need to devise a question for you to contemplate. For example, it could be 'what does taking responsibility for love in my life mean?' Or 'how would taking responsibility for love in my life look or feel like?' Settle on whatever question feels right for you, something that will give you insight into the idea.

Get into a comfortable position and gently relax your body by taking some deep breaths. Breathe into any area of your body that holds tension and as you breathe out feel the tension flowing out with your breath. Once you feel relaxed bring your breathing back to your normal rhythm and simply focus on your breath for a few minutes. At this point invite Grace into your contemplation in whatever way seems appropriate for you. Now ask yourself the question you wish to contemplate. Ask it three times and then simply sit and see what comes to mind. If you find your mind wandering, simply bring it back to the question. After sitting with the question for a while pick up your pen and begin to write. Let the answer flow, do not censor it, stop it or word-craft it. Simply allow your wisdom to emerge. Once you have finished, sit quietly for a moment and acknowledge the wisdom and insight received.

CHAPTER SEVEN

Practising Unconditional Love

Be the Love.

One way of practising unconditional love is to ask yourself the two questions that God asks in the book, *Conversations with God,* by Neale Donald Walsch. These questions are: 'what would love do now?' and 'is this who I am?' They are extremely powerful questions. To begin with asking these questions is living love. It brings love into our life on an everyday level. Love is who we really are, as we said it is our essence, our Self with the capital S. We are therefore asking, 'What would the Self do now?' 'What would the God within me do now?'

The two questions are inter-changeable. When you ask yourself the question, 'What would the Self do now?' the answer comes from the heart, bypasses the mind, skips to the left of the ego and appears immediately. That's how you know you can trust the answer. You haven't 'thought' it because it appears in a whole sentence. Imagine this: if I showed a film of a thought (from the ego) in slow motion it would show up word by word, like a sentence that comes on the screen as you type it. Whereas, however slow I make the film of an inspiration (from the heart) it would always show up complete – all the words appearing on screen at the same moment. Stop and sit for a moment and visualise the difference. This is one of the key understandings to the process of your ego/heart.

What would the Self do now?

The ego is very sneaky, once it realises that you can discern what is thought and what is inspiration it tries to confuse you and grab the inspiration and think it. However, because it is very proud of its sneakiness it will always try to improve it and this is your way of realising what's going on. One day I caught it embellishing an inspiration from the heart and realised that although it was really quick, it wasn't truth, it was an egoic thought – not inspiration. Stick to the original inspiration – the one that appeared in the moment and you'll be on course.

A typical time that this happens is when we are giving ourselves a hard time over something. We can be very good at beating ourselves up over what is actually a small matter. I can remember a time when I had to finish a set of guidelines for revision in a meeting and I was still miles off completion. I was getting tough on myself, berating myself for not finishing, wondering what everyone would think, when I remembered to ask myself, what would love do now, what would the Self do now? Immediately the solution came to me – to not worry what they would think (there was no way I could know that anyway) but to complete the outline as far as possible and then go to the group and ask for input. At that point my mind/ego thought it was a great idea if I could just add an extra section to the document so that it looked nearer the finished article, in other words, it would look better. Bingo, there it was – inspiration grabbed by ego and turned into thought! I went with the original inspiration and, with input from the whole group, the finished guidelines were much more thorough, clear and user-friendly.

It is these moments, when we touch in with our Self, that hold our truth. Our ego is always self-centred (small s) whereas our Self (large S) is God-centred. Truth comes from the source, from the heart, from God. It is always supportive of our highest intention and it is love. To come from the space of the Self, from unconditional love, benefits both ourselves and the rest of humanity. When we operate from unconditional love our lives feel much smoother. We stop judging so harshly, both others and ourselves. We offer help more readily as we are more sensitive to the needs of others in the moment. We are more in touch with our intuition; we simply know what is needed at any time. We step into a place of humanity by having more patience, understanding, compassion, empathy, integrity and joy and, by putting the world first, we not only serve others but ourselves too.

The true answer you get to the question 'what would love do now?' is often not what you'd think it would be. It will often fly in the face of the 'shoulds' – things we impose upon ourselves so that we will be loved. Now here's your next clue – true love is unconditional and therefore you don't need to do anything that is conditional. That's the purpose of the second question, 'is this who I am?' It's a great question; it really brings everything into focus and shows you your 'shoulds' and 'shouldn'ts'.

Many years ago I was reading a little booklet about being in a relationship. I had bought it as I had really wanted to be in a relationship and thought that this was the key. When I read the book I realised that it was actually about being in a relationship with myself. Imagine my disappointment! At the time I was into being a perfectionist and everything had to be done on time, by the book, in detriment to myself. Imagine my horror as I read that if you are sitting at your desk and don't know where to begin because you have so much to do and so little time to do it and you are feeling totally overwhelmed then get up, walk out the door and take the afternoon off. This blew me away.

The antidote to overwhelm.

The author's reasoning was that if we are in overwhelm, i.e. overwhelm is who you are, then we are not in touch with the flow of God, the flow of the Universe. Therefore we will not be efficient hands of God, God cannot flow through us in the form of work. We will be in the way and our fear of failure, fear of judgement and fear of losing love will stop the flow. The desire for love is the force that drives us; the fear of not getting it keeps our actions far from the place of unconditionality. Once you see, as in this example, that overwhelm is not who you are, it is so much easier to take a step back, let go of the 'shoulds' and follow your heart.

A few years ago I was working with someone who was in a similar situation. The feeling of overwhelm was huge and he was becoming unable to get anything done as his mind had jammed at the thought of what needed to be accomplished and what he had agreed to. With great resistance he left his desk to come and have a coffee and we talked about his situation and how he was feeling. After chatting for a while he began to see that pushing on through – trying to make it happen at all costs, even in detriment to his health – was not going to work. He saw that his fear of how he might be judged was clouding his better judgement of asking for help. He realised that he needed to create a realistic timeline rather than stick to the one that he had agreed to simply because of his fear. This was an action of unconditional love towards himself. By making the decision to deal honestly with the situation, both with himself and his company, it empowered him to come up with a viable solution. He felt more in touch with who he was (love) and was able to return to work without the fear. The company got back an efficient team member.

This 'getting back to who you are' can take on many forms. It can be very practical like in the example above or it can be more fluid as in taking time out to replenish yourself and get back in touch with the God within – be who you are. Sometimes it is as simple as sitting back and taking a deep breath and reconnecting with our-Selves. Love – God – wishes you to be who you are, hence the question 'what would the Self do now?' Love yourself unconditionally; all things come from that.

We've all heard this phrase 'love yourself' and it creates a myriad of reactions. These range from 'I do' – to 'simply not possible, I'm such a horrid person' – and many beliefs in between. In Deepak Chopra' book *The Path to Love* he talks about how we lose the infant's perspective of being completely loved and being completely lovable. Somewhere along the journey we have lost sight of these two truths. So, how do you love yourself? There are many levels to loving oneself and each moves us towards unconditional love. I see four practical ways; love yourself physically, emotionally, mentally and spiritually. They are not separate from each other but sometimes we are better at one than another.

Love Yourself Physically

One level is physical. To love oneself on the physical level is to take care of the body. In many traditions the body is likened to a temple. How often do you treat your body as a temple? Think about it. How would you look after your own temple? Wouldn't you treat it as a sacred place? With reverence, taking the time to ensure that it is as beautiful as possible? If your body is a temple then it is a place of worship. When you sit to meditate, to communicate with the divine within, that is a form of worship. How can you worship in a place that is not honoured?

It is therefore necessary to love and take care of your body. This can mean many things to many people and you have to decide what it means for you. For me it means taking regular exercise to ensure that my body is fit and healthy. Eating fresh, healthy foods and keeping to a nutritional plan that I know is right for my body. It means taking enough sleep to refresh me and give me energy for all I need to do. Having a balanced life so that I not only work, but play and relax and have time for meditation or simply some quiet time and just being. It is working out what is balance in my life and giving it to myself.

We also need to love our physicality. So often in our world we focus on the outside, the physical looks, how much we weigh, how we are perceived in the world. To love ourselves physically is to come to a place of loving acceptance of who we are, in our body, just as it is. We may want to make a few changes but it should not stop us loving ourselves. There is nothing more damaging than constantly berating ourselves because we are getting old, looking tired, overweight. When you think about it, how heavy is that negativity? What is it doing to your emotional and mental state? How loving is that? Instead, let's think of ourselves as beautiful, handsome, sexy, gorgeous, fun-loving, human beings.

Learn to love your physical self.

There will always be times when we get out of balance, when we do not love ourselves. Sometimes it will be a conscious decision, like the time I helped a friend with his business that involved working all night. Not getting my sleep is something that definitely doesn't help me, but I took the decision knowing this and afterwards I took some time to rest and recharge my batteries. I built a free day into my schedule so I could sleep in, and have an easy, quiet day afterwards. At other times it is not a conscious decision at all, it can be an addiction that kicks in and we go on some kind of a bender that is not loving at all – chocolate comes to mind. Whatever the situation, do not add to it by giving yourself a hard time, don't go on that guilt trip but simply re-dress the balance and come back to a space of loving yourself.

Loving Yourself Emotionally

To love yourself is also to love yourself emotionally. We all have our feelings, they are part of our makeup and we often have to work with our feelings around certain situations, people or occurrences. However, it makes life much easier if, as we work with our emotions, we see the polarities. For example happiness/sadness, anger/joy, love/fear, greed/generosity, bliss/pain. We can have a myriad of feelings and yes, we will need to work through them and look at the source of our reactions. However, remember that both polarities are equally valid. We need both to be able to experience the other. Without the sadness how would we know happiness? Without the love how would we know fear? As strange as it may seem we do need both to have the experience of all emotions on this human plane. With this in mind be easy on yourself and do not judge yourself for feeling emotional.

One way is to stop labelling any emotion 'good' or 'bad'. It is simply an emotion. Emotions need to flow through us. They are e-motion. Energy in motion. They cause us problems when we hang onto them and stop the flow of the energy. Depression can sometimes be caused by a suppression of emotions. A kind of deadening of all emotion so that we do not feel the one we are resisting. If you can embrace the emotion, love it as part of who you are, then it will be all the more easy to face it and release it from your life. What we resist about ourselves we actually create – by resisting something we are giving it energy and therefore keeping it in our life rather than letting it go. What we resist, persists. Loving your emotional makeup is another way of loving yourself.

There are times in my life when I have felt sad. Mostly there've been legitimate reasons for my sadness but even so, in the past I have felt that it has been wrong to be sad. I've judged the feeling of sadness and tried to stop the feeling or bury it deep within me. When my mother died, her death, and my process of grieving, taught me a great lesson. Sometimes we are sad. Plain and simple. Sadness is an emotion that we all feel. I tried to suppress the feeling and 'get on with life' and I did, on and off for a while, until I realised that in fact I had to let this energy flow through me.

Once I surrendered to the experience of grief I did, at times, feel a huge wave of sadness engulf me, crash over my head and I would find myself sobbing. After a while the sadness would dissipate and I would pick up and carry on with whatever I was doing. By allowing this process to flow – be in motion – I found that gradually the time between episodes of the sadness would lengthen until I got to the point that mostly I could sit and think about and appreciate her without feeling that huge sadness. Once I gave myself permission to allow the energy of sadness to flow, it flowed through me and out of my life. It can be useful at these times to give yourself a specific time in the day to create the space to feel for whatever you are feeling. This is especially good if you have a tendency to get stuck in sadness, it helps you remember that life does move on and there is a world outside your sorrow.

These experiences of letting ourselves go into emotion and truly feel it have a benefit of building our self-confidence. If we can allow ourselves to enter what may at the time feel like a black hole of sadness, and see that we do indeed come out the other side, we realise that we can deal with this level of emotion. That in turn shows us a depth of strength that we can pull on in challenging times. We begin to see just how strong we truly are and that we can and do meet any test that comes our way. We also come to know that next time it won't seem so daunting, a kind of 'been there, done that, got the T-shirt' feeling.

The same, full expression applies to the emotions we label as good. Some people don't let themselves feel too happy as they fear the downer that they think will surely come afterwards. So they limit their level of happiness, their level of enjoyment of everyday life. I can remember a scene in the film, *The Goodbye Girl,* from many years ago where the woman is pleading with the guy not to make her so happy, she didn't want to feel this good as she knew it would end. Don't limit your life in this way. Give yourself permission to revel in your happy times. Stop, be totally in the moment with them, relish them, allow the feelings to go through your body and know that these times can and will be repeated often. It is part of the rollercoaster of life.

So love your emotions, know that they are a unique part of you and know that if you consciously work with them, invite them in, accept and enjoy them all unconditionally, then you will be well on the way to becoming whole. Which, if you remember, was the point of unconditional love in the first place.

Loving your Mind

Loving your mental machinations is another facet to loving yourself. How many times have you thought to yourself, 'If only I could stop my mind saying XYZ.' 'Everything that happens is created by my mind and what a mess it has created.' The mind often gets much blame for the bad things that happen in our lives. 'If only I could turn off my mind I'd be able to meditate,' we often think to ourselves. The mind becomes the baddie in the woodpile, the instrument the ego uses to trick us into doing what 'it' wants.

We do need to watch the mind as it does have the capacity to create things. Both our repetitive negative thoughts as well as the positive ones are affirmations that help to create our world. But it is necessary to love the mind, to befriend the mind. By loving the mind we gradually make friends with it and in making friends with it we can be aware of our thoughts.

When we become aware of what we are thinking, it brings you into the present and that is the place you make choices. Then we can consciously change our thinking, change our attitude. We can only do this when we are on the same side as the mind, if it is a battle then the mind will always win. Don't battle your mind, don't create a war with your ego – love your mind, thank your mind for its incredible capacity and begin the road to awareness.

I remember once when I was in the ashram in upstate New York, I was listening to a talk given by one of the monks who had studied the mind for many years. He wrote a book called, *What's on my Mind,* and he was giving a course called 'Calling the Ego's Bluff'. He talked about befriending the mind and said that he had realised that we are hard on the mind sometimes.

He had been trying to remember a particular way of being and had been praying for this constant remembrance.

As we all do, he sometimes forgot and when he got around to remembering he gave his mind a hard time for forgetting! He came to realise that in fact he was reinforcing his forgetfulness by this behaviour. He said if you constantly told off a child for reminding you of something, in the end the child would not come to remind you. It will not want the telling off. In the same way each time we berate ourselves for forgetting we are telling the mind not to remind us in the future or we will tell it off.

It doesn't matter what it is you are trying to remember. It could be remembering to buy washing powder next time you are in the supermarket or deciding that you no longer wish to go over a specific event in your mind. Instead of berating our mind, the monk suggested thanking the mind when it remembers, practise gratitude for the remembrance and then the mind will be encouraged to remember more readily in the future. This is a great way to love your mind. Make it an actual practise, just start one day at a time. Make an agreement with yourself, 'today whenever I remember something I will thank my mind'.

I was reading a newspaper article on happiness recently. It had concluded that from the days when we lived in complete survival mode, our cave man era, we had set up neural pathways that kept us alert to anything being wrong. In those days if we noticed quickly enough that something was amiss, we could take action and therefore keep on surviving. In fact, we had set up six main neural pathways for noticing something wrong and only one for noticing joy. In those days joy was fleeting and it didn't keep you alive. We still have these neural pathways in place. Think about it, how often does your mind go to find something wrong rather than something right? We are programmed to notice things that are wrong. The nice thing is that we can create new neural pathways. By learning to actually thank yourself for remembering something, we create a new pathway of noticing something positive. In the film, *What the Bleep do We Know?* it explains that if we stop using old neural pathways , i.e. stop noticing the bad and begin to notice the good, then new pathways are set up and the old disconnect from disuse. This illustrates the science behind the NLP processes we talked of earlier and one of the reasons why it is so effective.

By loving your mind you get an ally on your side. Your ability to practise unconditional love will be greater as you will be more mindful in each interaction you have with the world.

Loving your Self

And finally – love your Self. This is the final part of loving yourself. Love the essence of who you are. Love the spiritual journey you are on and where you are on that journey. Love the one within that guides you constantly. Take the time to be with your Self. Ensure that you have times of silence in your day to tune in and be with your Self. Give time to allow a connection with the divine on a daily basis. This may take many forms and only you will know what works best for you. Experiment until you have found a way to be with God. Try different methods – sometimes I find chanting brings me close, especially when my mind is busy and to meditate feels like I am creating a shopping list. Other days a long walk in a beautiful place reconnects me to the divine.

We all need to have some time with ourselves. It doesn't matter how you label it; meditation, prayer, silence, quiet time, a solitary walk, the result is the same. Think back to something that you have done that gives you a feeling of peace inside. Sometimes it can be as simple as a long, hot bath. A feeling of coming back to yourself. In our busy lives we often forget to give ourselves some downtime. Look at your daily schedule, where would it best for you to have some time to yourself? A likely time is early morning, especially if you have a partner and family who fill the rest of your day, but the choice is yours. Give yourself just 30 minutes in your day, or more if you'd like, the rest of the day will be much smoother.

A client told me recently that since she has been practising meditation each morning she has found she can handle the world with much more poise and calm. Her busy job doesn't throw her off so much and she is far nicer with her family after a full day's work. In other words she is able to practise a greater level of unconditional love. What can you do in your precious 30 minutes?

Loving unconditionally, warts and all, is a way towards becoming whole. By embracing all that you are you can start to change things that no longer serve you. You can begin to interact with those around you in a new and loving way. Your life will begin to feel more harmonious. You will be more in tune with your heart and intuition. Starting with yourself – you can be the love you wish to give and receive. Loving yourself is not the ego trip kind of love, the 'I am great in the eyes of the world and others'. It is the quiet, unassuming acceptance of who you are right now. With this much love in your life it is a definite move towards Remembering Perfection.

Tips

- To start recognising true inspiration ask yourself – did the words appear on the screen all at the same time (inspiration) or did I think them one by one (thought).

- If you find yourself rewording and/or improving an inspiration then that is a sure sign it was an inspirational hit. Stick to the original – that's your truth.

- When you are feeling hassled, stop. Ask yourself, am I coming from love? Is this hassle who I am?

- Create a list of things that you can do to redress the balance when you are out of sorts physically. These may be restful, like a massage or a long hot bath, or more physical like taking a walk, swimming, or doing some yoga. What helps you redress the physical balance? Make an intention to do one of these things whenever you feel out of kilter.

- When you catch yourself avoiding or suppressing an uncomfortable emotion take some time and space and delve into it, allow yourself to feel it and allow it to flow through you. You may wish to do this alone or with someone you trust as a support. Learn to love your emotions.

- Make an agreement with yourself, 'today whenever I remember something I will thank my mind'. Make it an actual practise of gratitude, simply start one day at a time. Befriend your mind and by doing so it will become your ally.

- Set times in your day to be with the divine. Those precious 30 minutes. Be it meditation, a walk in the woods, listening to music, prayer. Identify different ways this may take place, things that work for you. If inside, create a sacred space in your home, a place that holds the energy of love – it may be simply a specific chair – know that you have a place you can go to anytime to reconnect with the God – Love within.

Contemplation

Give yourself at least half an hour for this contemplation. If you have a place within your home where you meditate use this space, or if not just find somewhere quiet where you will not be disturbed. Have your journal or a notebook handy.

Before you start this contemplation identify one idea or phrase that stood out for you in this chapter. For example, it might be the idea of loving yourself emotionally. Now devise a question for you to contemplate. For example, it could be 'how can I love myself emotionally?' Or 'how could I remember to love unconditionally?' Settle on whatever question feels right for you, something that will give you insight.

Get into a comfortable position and gently relax your body by taking some deep breaths. Breathe into any area of your body that holds tension and as you breathe out feel the tension flowing out with your breath. Once you feel relaxed bring your breathing back to your normal rhythm and simply focus on your breath for a few minutes. At this point invite Grace into your contemplation in whatever way seems appropriate for you. Now ask yourself the question you wish to contemplate. Ask it three times and then simply sit and see what comes to mind. If you find your mind wandering simply bring it back to the question. After sitting with the question for a while pick up your pen and begin to write. Let the answer flow, do not censor it, stop it or word-craft it. Simply allow your wisdom to emerge. Once you have finished sit quietly for a moment and acknowledge the wisdom and insight.

CHAPTER EIGHT

Intuition

The constant guide within.

What is intuition? How do we develop it? How do we characterise it, know it, trust it? These questions are just a few that are often asked in connection with intuition. The dictionary definition states: 'a faculty of consciousness directed by unreasoning feeling or instinct, characterised by immediate perception.' This may sound a bit wordy but as a definition it has most of the requisite parts of how I would define intuition. Intuition is not something outside of us, it is a part of our own consciousness. It is a connection with the God within, which in turn is part of the universal consciousness. It is often without logic, the unreasoning feeling, and has no proof of its rightness. And yet it always comes with a feeling of clarity, an immediate knowing. If that is the case, why do we so often ignore our intuitive hits? Why is it that we think we know best, or better?

Our intuition can scare us silly. It often goes against what we think is the safe option. It is a constant, always guiding us, but often we don't like what it is telling us. It goes against what we think is right, or it can feel downright dangerous. Our intuition differs from our instinct in that instinct is tied to our survival whereas intuition always presents us with a choice. We have all heard of the flight or fight level of survival, the one that tells us to jump out the way if a car is heading towards us. That reaction is not a thinking activity, it is pure instinct. Intuition on the other hand allows us choice. The clearest example I know of is when we are physically attracted to someone but our inner voice is telling us that no way is this good for you. The instinct, the purely chemical reaction to another human being, has no cognitive thought process to it; it is pure animal. The intuition, which tells us 'no way', then gives us the choice; do we follow the physical or listen to the higher wisdom within?

Intuition always presents us with choice, whether we can hear it is up to us.

We have free will as to whether we listen and act on our intuition. Do we listen, do we like what we hear? Is it safe? Will everything work out ok if I follow its prompting? The largest factor in this ability to listen and follow is our self-esteem. Are we strong enough to follow a guidance that may, more often than not, guide us to do or say something that goes against either our wishes (survival/safety) or the societal norm? In this chapter we will explore the differing facets of intuition, how we can hear it and learn to act on it.

Who is Intuitive?

We all are. We all have the capacity to be intuitive. Whether we hear it is a different matter. When I explore intuitive capacity with my clients I often come across people saying, 'oh no, I'm not intuitive at all. I never receive guidance like that'. I dispute this. On exploration almost everyone will admit that they have, at times, known to do or not to do something. They have had a feeling within themselves, sometimes even physical, and they have not listened to it. On reflection they have admitted to themselves, if not to others, that actually they knew what to do, they had a feeling but they ignored it. That is their intuitive voice.

I was recently in London and staying with a friend. On my previous visit I had realised that the local tube station sometimes closed the escalators so on that occasion I had used another station as I had a heavy suitcase. This time, on the day I was leaving, I remembered about the escalators but immediately dismissed it. My mind knew better, hadn't I seen them working only yesterday? Sure as eggs are eggs they were closed and I ended up carrying my suitcase down 110 steps. This was a classic example of me ignoring my intuitive voice. It is also a good example that we are constantly given guidance on the most mundane things. Our intuition is not just for the big issues in our lives. If we allow the voice room then we can be guided throughout our day.

It doesn't have to be spooky, otherworldly. If we start to notice, we find we are actually guided on everything, it is simply a matter of using our higher intelligence in conjunction with our everyday mind. As humans we have a large mental capacity that is unused. This is scientific fact. I believe our intuitive function is part of this unused capacity, and we become very competent beings when we hear our intuitive voice and follow that input using our normal mental capacity. There will always be an element of thinking in everything we do, the trick is to be open enough to hear our guidance before our minds kick in, and then have the strength to act on it. One of my favourite sayings that reminds me to listen is, 'if it comes to your attention, give it your attention'.

In the past the intuitive voice was valued and not thought to be anything special, it simply was. I have a friend whose grandmother, who lived in Southern Ireland in the early part of the last century, was the proverbial wise woman and healer. Not only did the local people seek and respect her opinion about problems, they would come to her for healing too. For her it was nothing special, simply how she was and operated in the world. This way of living was the norm until only relatively recently. In all the different ancient cultures intuition was honoured and called forth. The Elders in the Native American tribe, the Guru in India, the Lama in Tibet, the Shaman in South America are but a few that are still honoured to this day. In the past not only were these individual people honoured for their role, but living from your intuition was normal for everyone. Native Americans say someone who is 'thinking with their head' (not their heart) as a way of indicating they've gone crazy! It is this ingrained way of being that we, particularly in the western world, have lost.

OH NO! HE'S THINKING AGAIN...

As time moved on our western society stopped valuing this way of being. Logical thought was prized to the exclusion of all other. I once worked at an environmental agency that was in touch with many intuitive inventors. People who woke up one day simply knowing how something worked and then set out to build or create it. Some of these inventions were revolutionary, they worked but could not be scientifically explained. For example, one was a product that cleaned sewage water using properties similar to homeopathy. When it was tested in the laboratory it tested as pure water. When we tried to get funding for these types of projects the one barrier that seemed to be present was that there was no logical explanation or research set down. It felt to us that if the inventors had been able to show a seven-year research project then funding would be forthcoming. Without that proof of logical, sequential thought and scientific experimentation it was impossible. I like the quote from Albert Einstein, 'We can't solve problems by using the same kind of thinking we used when we created them.' He saw that we needed to go beyond the logical mind for our solutions.

However, the tide is slowly turning. People in business are beginning to realise that without the space for intuitive perception we are losing a valuable asset. As Nancy Kline says in her book, *Time to Think*, it is often in a thinking environment where each individual in a group is given the time and space to find the answers within which the best solutions lay. Science after all has used the intuitive mind as a fount of inspiration, we all know the Eureka moment, why not value it in all sectors of life? Now is a moment when we can all start the journey back to using our higher intelligence in all aspects of our life. To live guided by that part of ourselves that is the God within. Intuition is back in favour and about time too!

How can we use Intuition in our Lives?

So how do we open ourselves to our intuition? How do we begin to be guided? We can choose to be open to our intuition, but it's not a case of simply stating it and hey presto we are constantly guided. Rather the first step is to build our self-esteem. We have to learn to like ourselves and feel the confidence to follow our hunches. If we are not strong enough in our self-belief then we are not going to be able to hear what our intuition is guiding us to do, especially if it is life changing.

To help us find the courage to listen to the big hits, try listening and noticing the small, everyday ones, first. The ones that tell us to call a friend now, or go back and pick up the cheque book we've left behind. This is intuition too, and if we create an intention to be more vigilant and listen to it then we gain confidence. This confidence will then help us as we start to live with and follow our guidance for the bigger hits. Again – if it comes to your attention, give it your attention.

Often when we ask for guidance in our lives the answer is not to our liking, or makes us feel doubtful. It may feel illogical and unsafe. It definitely does not come with guarantees of safety. The 'do this and everything will be ok' guidance doesn't exist at this level of being. But ask yourself 'Who needs this safety?' In reality it is our ego that needs the safety. Our Self is champing at the bit for us to follow as much guidance as we can hear. It is always our ego that holds us back for fear of the change that it may bring. On one level we know that if we really let off the brakes and lived in the moment, following our intuition, then our learning in this lifetime would progress at a very fast pace. This is the acceleration the ego shuns. If we truly come to know through our life experience that we are not separate from each other then the ego is no longer in control. This is why we have the constant critical inner voice within holding us back, keeping us 'safe'. However, even if we throw safety to the wind and commit to following our intuition we still need to know how to feel and hear it.

What does it feel like, how do you recognise this intuitive hit? For each person it is different, for many it is accompanied by a physical sensation. It might be a warmth in the heart region, a strong sensation like excitement in the gut – the good old gut reaction. Some people get goose bumps, or a shiver down their spine. Others simply know, almost like they have been instantly downloaded with information. As you begin to open to your intuition you will start to notice the signs that are peculiar to you, and these then become your intuition alarm. One thing that many people will say is that it feels very clear, not something half thought out, but an absolute clarity. It also helps if we work to clear the mind. Meditation is a powerful tool here. As Swami Durgananda points out in her book *The Heart of Meditation*, one of the major gifts of meditation is its power to clear the mind. When you have a clear mind you can hear your intuitive voice.

You need an inner strength to be able to listen to and follow a voice that suggests you do something that not only feels out of your comfort zone, but will most likely make no sense to those around you. Following the intuitive voice will move you from keeping in line with the collective conscious idea, (or as Caroline Myss calls it 'the tribal mind'), to making conscious, individual choices. Once you know this, you have a pretty good pointer on whether you are on the right track. If it feels exciting or maybe scary, not logical, perhaps pushing against all your safety boundaries and yet it still feels 'right', then you have heard an intuitive guidance. The next choice is to follow it.

One small pointer at this stage, beware of pushing yourself beyond your comfort zone into the zone of fear. As we have said before, whenever we make decisions and take steps forward we also need to be aware of our energy behind something. Therefore, if you get an intuitive hit that scares you, the first thing to do is ascertain what fear pattern it is hitting. At that point you can ask yourself if this truly is guidance or do you just think it is. Once you know for sure that it is the right action, you need to address the fear first. Take a close look at what it is you are frightened of, and work to lessen the fear as we've discussed earlier, until you are in a place where you move forward from a calm positive place. You may not dismiss the fear altogether but it should no longer be the sponsoring energy with which you take steps. The sponsoring energy is excitement. As we learn to apply our spirituality in our everyday life these situations will occur. We will be guided and often it will mean that we address our fears, it is part of the journey and it this that brings us closer to our true Self.

A few years ago, when I went to India, I had this experience of fear arise. I was due to go to visit the ashram for the first time and illogically I felt that I had to resign my job before I went. It was such a strong feeling. However, up until that time, I had never taken a chance in my working life. I had always had some new job to go to. The idea of resigning without knowing where I'd get another job was huge, crazy. I procrastinated for a long while, but eventually, after taking a look at my fear, I realised that it was unfounded. With my experience and qualifications I logically knew I would work again. Even so with some trepidation and confusion, 'why was I doing this?' I resigned.

My friend who I worked for said that she knew the moment I walked into the office what was going to happen because I looked fifteen years younger. The stress of holding out against the strong intuition had shown. A month later I went to the ashram. I had no idea when I took off from Heathrow just how life-changing this experience was going to be. After three days I got another very strong hit that I needed to stay more than two weeks. In fact, I needed to stay three months. Now I realised the 'why'. If I hadn't resigned my job and tidied up the loose ends there was no way I could have stayed. By following my intuition, even though the idea scared me, my life changed totally – and for the better.

Following your intuition can, and mostly likely will, lead you to places you wouldn't have thought of going. Doing things that are outside your normal way of being. If someone had told me a year earlier I would resign my job and go to India to visit an ashram I would have thought them crazy. However, from my own experience, I can only encourage you to open yourself to this stream of guidance and work towards being strong enough to follow it. Life is an adventure, an Earth School playground where we learn who we are and what we are here for. Our intuition will guide us to all the best experiences if we simply have enough guts to let it.

Intuition and Self-Esteem

This is where a strong self-esteem comes in. If you do not feel good about yourself, like yourself and are able to stand up for your decisions, then you will not be able to follow your guidance. Self-esteem has many layers. First we have our bodily self-esteem. How we look and how we feel in the world. I was watching a program on TV recently called *Spirituality Shopper*. In it a woman was given four different spiritual practises that would hopefully give her a greater feeling of fulfilment in her life. One of the practises was Christian Lent in which she was challenged to give up something, and she chose her hair straighteners. She normally spent half an hour a day straightening her hair, it was an important ritual to her so she would feel confident and presentable in the world. The first two weeks of curly hair was very challenging for her. However, by the end of the month she had gained in confidence so much that she could embrace who she was, curly hair and all and decided to stay with the natural look. Everyone thought she looked much more natural, more like her. Her self-esteem had grown, simply by practising being herself, hair and all. That, along with the positive feedback she received, changed her perception of herself in the world. It was a beautiful example of growing self-esteem.

The next level of self-esteem is our intellectual self-esteem. This is influenced by our experience in the world, how we think and how others judge us in our thinking. A child constantly labelled as stupid in school will seldom, without much help, be someone who will put forward new and challenging ideas. They will play safe and only put themselves forward if they feel secure enough in what they are saying. Good teachers can help build the intellectual self-esteem of children. In an experiment, a new teacher at a school was told that her class were all very bright and that she could expect higher than average marks for their age group.

Sure enough by the end of the term they were all getting above average marks even though in truth they were simply an ordinary mix of kids.

It was the way that the teacher treated them, expecting them to do well, pushing their boundaries with her understanding of what she thought their abilities were, that allowed the children's intellectual self-esteem to rise. In doing so, they began to expect more of themselves, used their abilities to a greater degree and excelled. A strong intellectual self-esteem is very important in being able to follow our intuition. If we cannot feel confident amongst our intellectual peers what hope do we have in following our truth. It is those peers, who may feel threatened by our change, that we will have to stand up against. By valuing our intellect and learning that our opinions and thoughts count, we become strong enough to act on our intuition.

Emotional self-esteem is another area that many fall down in. This is ability to handle your emotions and not allow others to manipulate you through them. The need to be able to both protect yourself and to provide for yourself emotionally. As we saw in the chapter about unconditional love it is normal in our western world to judge our emotions. If we feel sad, angry, envious, we think that these are bad. If we feel happy, joyful, loving, we think that these are good. In truth they are all simply emotional states. We will all at some time in our lives feel the full range of emotions. One way to build our emotional self-esteem is to begin to accept that we are emotional beings and that judging these emotions to be good or bad does not support us in handling what we are feeling.

> THIS ONE'S NO GOOD...

Don't judge your emotions.

When we are feeling down we often feel worse if we fight the emotion. We think we shouldn't feel like this. We fight the reality of the feeling. But as Byron Katie asks in her book, *Loving What Is*, can you absolutely know that to be true? Is it absolutely true when we say that we shouldn't be feeling like this? Because, in all reality, it is how we are feeling. Why fight with reality? Therefore if we can simply allow ourselves to feel whatever it is, it will move through us far easier. The old adage 'what you resist, persists', especially when sad or angry emotions are in play.

It is also true that we are afraid of our emotions. Part of us believes that if we allow our sad emotions free reign then maybe we will never stop crying. I have news for you – no-one has never not been able to stop crying. We fear going into our emotions for fear of being judged weak, soft, or unstable. To build our emotional self-esteem we need to begin to learn to trust them as simple expressions of how we feel at any particular time. To listen to them and not resist them. The old days of people telling us not to cry when we are upset need to be banished. By not resisting the emotion you are far more likely to feel better anyway, the emotion can just move through you and out – don't we all feel better after a good cry? Choose carefully who you have around you, a true supporter is someone who allows you to feel what you are feeling without trying to change it at all. If you are sad, allow sadness just as if you are deliriously happy – allow that too.

It may seem odd to say allow yourself to be deliriously happy but there are some in the world who limit their expressions and revelling in joy. They come from the 'if I get really happy I may lose it and then I'll feel sad so it's better not to feel too good' school of thought. Emotional self-esteem is knowing that you can handle the full spectrum.

As we learn to honour our feelings and know that it is ok to feel, our self-esteem grows. We come out the other side of an emotional situation feeling stronger and more able to cope in those situations. The feeling of autonomy grows and with it the ability to listen to the guidance in our lives. If we know that we can handle any emotional situation that comes our way, we don't hesitate to follow our intuition. So often we procrastinate because we don't know how we will cope with the outcome of doing something outside our normal way of being. By being strong emotionally we can wipe this fear aside, we become invincible, a true spiritual warrior flowing forth on our unique spiritual quest.

As we build our levels of self-esteem in the physical world we also build our levels of spiritual or intuitive self-esteem. We come to know that our spirit only has the boundaries that we level on it. As we become stronger in knowing who we are and feeling free from the tribal constraints of what we should do, we begin to see that it is only ourselves that limit our way of being. Our intuition, our ability to listen to our higher self, our guidance, is only limited by our fear, our lack of self-esteem in standing out and being different. It is our basic fear of survival that keeps us stuck, stops us following our intuition. Our Soul has no desire to take us back to a place where our ego is back in charge of our survival. Our Soul needs us to be free to do its bidding as much as it needs the ego's power to create.

When I returned to Europe after living in the ashram in the States for four years I tried very hard to conform back into my old way of life, rejoin the old 'tribe'. I thought it felt safe even if it did feel rather constricting. Whilst taking some time out in Spain before going back to London to rejoin the corporate world many different ideas and opportunities presented themselves. Part of me, my Soul, was straining at the bit to jump into these seemingly illogical options. Come and live in Spain, follow the dream, jump out of the mainstream, follow your heart. It felt like I needed to be in Spain, but I didn't know why. All the while I was trying to think of a way I could have the dream abroad but still live safe in the London world. But as a friend pointed out, I would spend all my time in London trying to support a life in Spain I wasn't living. The many foreign-owned villas that were used only four weeks of the year attested to that. Still I was fearful to make the jump that inside I was aching to do.

We already had many physical supports for the move, a place to live, an offer of some work, but I felt afraid and confused all the same so I asked for guidance from within. We were driving back from visiting Granada and in the quiet of the drive I had a clear strong voice inside say – 'Did you really think you could go back to the old way of living?' It was such a powerful feeling, a 'get real' moment, that all fear dropped away. I realised that never again could I take the safe road and ignore the intuition that guided me. I saw that life, lived fully, had no guarantees, only experiences that constantly taught me to grow, push the comfort-zone boundary and live life to the fullest.

Living and hearing your intuition is not miraculous. For each of us it can and should become an everyday occurrence. By practising acting on our intuitive hits, small ones at first to build our confidence, we start to move from thinking our life to perceiving our life. As I work with clients I often start by asking them how they feel about something as this takes them out of the realm of their thoughts. Our intuition often comes with a physical feeling, the gut reactions, the heartfelt knowing, the rush of excitement or nervousness. If you want to perceive your world, then feel it first.

When you want clarity, ask yourself, 'how do I feel about this?' Forgetting all the 'shoulds' and 'coulds'– what do I feel is the right course of action? Sometimes our minds will block this line of enquiry and so it is useful to ask the question and then drop it. Know that at some point the answer will come, most likely when the mind and ego has dropped its guard. Meditation is good for aiding us to hear the intuitive voice. Not necessarily in meditation but the action of quietening the chaos inside can allow the small voice to be heard at other times too.

A good friend of mine was caught in a life-and-death situation in which the solid knowing and trust of the voice inside saved his life. He was in Africa working for an NGO aid agency and, as is the case in many situations, getting too close to the militia who did not want the status quo to change. They decided to kill him and took him out into the desert where they aimed a gun at him and started shooting. He ran into some undulating dunes as they continued to fire. He was hit and as he was about to get up and run some more a voice inside him instructed him to stay still. This instruction went against all his instinctual responses of flight. Luckily he trusted his voice even though it seemed totally illogical to do so. They assumed he was dead and drove off. He lived to tell the tale.

Now this is an extreme example but it does illustrate two points. One, he had enough experience and self-esteem to listen to that inner voice. Two, intuitive guidance rarely conforms to what we think it should. It comes with no guarantees except one: you have a karmic destiny to fulfil. Your intuition will guide you through the fastest route, you may meet so-called disasters, but you would have met them anyway in some form or another. Our Soul has one calling only, it moves us towards the place of enlightenment, to merge back into the whole, back into God. Intuition will fast-track us and give us the experiences we need to fulfil our own personal destiny.

In truth what else can you rely on? Who else other than your higher self has your best interests at heart? As we grow in self-esteem we begin to see that this is true. Once we are strong enough to stand by ourselves in all areas of our lives, physically, intellectually, emotionally and spiritually, we see that our connection with the divine is through our own intuition.

Seen from the outside, a life lived with intuitive guidance may seem haphazard, full of mistakes, with no plan. We will never know the reason why some things happen and, in fact, that is not the point. The point is that we learn that there is something higher, greater than our small, limited ego, something that, if we allow, can run the most amazing show on earth – life at full volume. Life lived in the flow, no grasping at the river bank but in the middle of the current. A life that teaches us who we are, what our truth is. A life that is more alive with purpose than we can imagine. A life where we learn to trust our intuition and know that it will lead us where we need to go. It may not give us what we think we want but it will fulfil our spiritual needs.

Following your intuition means living Life at full volume.

As we build our self-esteem to a point where we begin to hear, trust and live by our intuition, the other spiritual principles we aspire to live by become more second nature to us. Our intuition will always guide us to be loving, to see God in each other, to practise gratitude. By being real we will invite our intuition in and it will guide us when we create our reality, and remind us that it is our attitude that is important in relation to what is happening in our life. Intuition becomes our guiding light, and we learn that to follow our intuition is the highest form of taking responsibility for our lives, and the way towards Remembering Perfection.

Tips

- As you start to practise to use your intuition make a point to notice at the end of each day – which hits did I follow, which hits did I ignore? Become more aware of how intuition works in your life.

- Imbibe this: if it comes to your attention, give it your attention.

- When we ask for guidance at least give the answer the time of day even if you don't like it. Often the best options are disguised as the crazy ones.

- Intuitive guidance will often lead you away from the tribal norm. If it feels scary, not logical, against all your safety boundaries and yet it still feels 'right' then you have heard an intuitive guidance. The next choice is – do you want to follow it?

- Always address any fear that is raised by an intuitive hit. Fear should never be the sponsoring energy when following intuition (or anything else for that matter).

- Take an honest look at your self-esteem. Do you like who you are? Do you respect you? How would you rate your self-esteem – intellectually, emotionally, physically and spiritually. Identify one thing you can do to start addressing the balance.

- Learn to perceive your life, feel it. If you want guidance ask 'what do I feel about this?' Your body will always take you out of the realm of your mind, use it.

- Meditate! You know it's good for you.

Contemplation

Give yourself at least half an hour for this contemplation. If you have a place within your home where you meditate use this space or if not just find somewhere quiet where you will not be disturbed. Have your journal or a notebook handy.

Before you start this contemplation identify one idea or phrase that stood out for you in this chapter. For example, it might be the idea of feeling your intuition in your body. You now need to devise a question for you to contemplate. For example, it could be 'how will I know when I feel an intuitive hit?' Or 'how can I become more open to feel my intuition?' Settle on whatever question feels right for you, something that will give you insight.

Get into a comfortable position and gently relax your body by taking some deep breaths. Breathe into any area of your body that holds tension and as you breathe out feel the tension flowing out with your breath. Once you are relaxed bring your breathing back to your normal rhythm and simply focus on your breath for a few minutes. At this point invite Grace into your contemplation in whatever way seems appropriate for you. Now ask yourself the question you wish to contemplate. Ask it three times and then simply sit and see what comes to mind. If you find your mind wandering simply bring it back to the question. After sitting with the question for a while pick up your pen and begin to write. Let the answer flow, do not censor it, stop it or word-craft it. Simply allow your wisdom to emerge. Once you have finished sit quietly for a moment and acknowledge the wisdom and insight received.

CHAPTER NINE

Trust and Faith

Not as in blind faith but a faith nurtured through our inner experience.

To live our lives with a spiritual perspective we need to trust and to have faith. Sometimes this is the hardest part of applying spirituality in our everyday life. How can we trust when things are seemingly out of control? How can we have faith when we don't know what is going to happen next or if it is going to work out all right? But, without both trust and faith we are unable to relax into our lives. We worry; we try to make sure everything has our desired outcome. We forget that we are in a much bigger play than we can ever imagine, we are in God's play and we are the actors on the stage. Sometimes, in fact a lot of the time, we buy into the illusion of life, the seriousness of life, we think that we are in control.

I have known people balk at the idea of having faith, of trusting in God, in destiny. They feel it is a way of abdicating responsibility as well as handing over control. To them it smacks of opting out of life, of people using the idea that if everything happens because of God then they don't have to do anything. It feels like using this as an excuse for not making something of themselves. This standpoint is understandable simply because it is a misunderstanding of what true trust and faith are about.

In this chapter we will explore not only the meaning of trust and faith but how they operate in our lives. We will look at how we build them and why they make our lives flow more easily. And we will see how we can relax into living rather than always be worried about what might be around the corner. We will come to see that we can only apply our spirituality in our lives when we have the faith that life works.

What is Trust and Faith?

Trust and faith indicates that there is something bigger than us, something greater that has a role in our destiny. It infers that we actually have a destiny, that we play a part in the bigger picture of the Universe. To those who are mired in their separateness it can be a threatening thought. It can be scary that something other than ourselves can create situations in our lives. Then add the dimension that this 'thing' is intangible and you will begin to see why people have so much trouble trusting in God. There is also the fear that if we put our trust in this 'something', what if it turns out to be a nothing? How silly will we look then? How awful if we've put all our trust in something we believe and then it turns out to be wrong?

I had been living in the ashram in upstate New York for about two years when I had a similar crisis of faith. For days I walked around with this voice in my head saying, 'what if you are wrong? What if all this spirituality stuff is a hoax? What if there is no Self? What if the idea of oneness isn't true? What if when you die you simply disappear? What about reincarnation, the different dimension that we go to when we die? What if it is all a delusion?' After a few panicky days stuck in this cycle of doubt, I began to see that this was the ego's voice. The closer we come to our spiritual truths, the harder the ego will fight to discredit them. It has no desire for us to follow our Soul's desire, rather it would keep us back in the mire of illusion. However, not only was this a play of the ego, but it was also a part of the spiritual path. We are meant to question and doubt everything because in this way we deepen our connection to what is the truth for us, and discard what is not. The mind is not only the cause of all suffering but also the cause of liberation. This questioning is actually how we move into a place of trust, how we learn to have faith.

St John of the Cross, the Christian Saint, called this time of doubt the dark night of the Soul. It is a time of spiritual madness, when we come to question all that we believe. Often it is tied into a time when all our points of reference are being torn away from us. We may feel abandoned both by the world as we know it and by God. A time of crying inside, 'what is happening to my life, why am I feeling so wretched?' These times of spiritual madness are a necessary transition time as one set of paradigms is exchanged for another. As we start to examine our spiritual beliefs, our outer world shifts out of focus and we are lost in a fog wondering why we have been forsaken. At times like these our trust and faith are tested to the extreme. Get excited – you are on the brink of an insight.

I know someone who, within one month of her mother dying, also lost her business. Her distress and grief were huge but at the same time she knew that her faith was being tested. She continued with her spiritual practise, prayed for support, and the calmness she found within gave her the strength to continue. A year later she herself said that her experience of that time had changed her, deepened her connection to Source, to God within, and strengthened her faith in the process called life. By coming through the experience and becoming strong, it confirmed her faith and trust. If we have challenging situations like these we are also being asked to have faith. To trust that everything is as it should be even though we may feel so unconnected that we might as well be living on a desert island. It may not be obvious, but even in these times it is exactly as it should be.

As the dark night surrounds us we must not fight it. Once again, 'what you resist, persists' is in motion here. Relax into the fog, allow it to envelop you, take time to explore what is there through meditation or contemplation and know that you will come out the other side. Another invaluable support is to have a spiritual mentor or friend. This person, or persons if you have a support group, needs to be like-minded and more importantly, is not there to give you answers. They are there to listen and simply be with you through your process. You are the only one who has your answers and explanations, but by having someone with you as you evolve helps validate the experiences. It is as it should be, nothing is wrong.

We have all had the experience of needing to talk. The simple act of speaking helps us get things clear. At times it may be a specific person we need to talk to, but often it is simply a matter of finding someone who will understand and listen. Someone who understands how we think. Who will ask pertinent questions to help us get a clearer view of where we stand in our life. This is the role of the spiritual mentor or support group. They are not there to fix our situation but are people we can feel connected to and heard by and they play an important role in our lives, whether it be spiritually or worldly.

'Night is always darkest before the dawn' is a true proverb. Something revolutionary always comes out of these experiences, sometimes in a quiet 'ah-ha' insight and sometimes in a brilliant flash of inspiration. Just know that our times of spiritual madness (note I said times, as they happen more than once in our lives) are transitory and highly beneficial.

As I began to emerge from my dark days during my time in the ashram, I started to look at each of the questions that arose in my mind. I began to see that I had had experiences that countered the doubt. I had experienced the still place within in meditation. I had touched the Self and felt the bliss of oneness.

I had explored reincarnation and past lives and known them to be true. And, illogically, when I questioned my beliefs I simply could not imagine making an ounce of sense of our world without there being a spiritual explanation. Without the goal of our spiritual life, enlightenment, and the experiences and lessons that lead us there, what is this all for? By having this very unsettling experience not only had my faith deepened, I felt I could carry my spirituality into my life in a more integrated way. My crisis of faith, my dark night had dawned into a new way of living.

So many people nowadays are looking at their very material lives and asking themselves what is this life for? There must be something more than this. This question arises from within, and the lack of faith is an inner hole that for everyone, at some time in some lifetime, refuses to go away. Only a greater goal, a greater purpose, makes sense of the lessons we are learning. Life without the trust and faith it takes to live a spiritual life is, in the long run, empty and meaningless. I speak to many people through my coaching practise who come to me because they wish to change something in their outer lives. It is no co-incidence that they come to me, a person who gives inner life equal if not greater importance. More often than not they are looking for something of greater meaning in their lives. They may start the process in the material world but sooner or later 95% of them start to talk about feeling empty, unfulfilled even with their successes. Only then do we start to talk about balancing life, purpose, spirituality and what it means. Developing trust and the resulting faith are an integral part of the journey.

Who, What to Trust?

So who is it that we trust? What are we trusting? The first 'who' we need to trust is ourselves. As with intuition this takes a healthy self-esteem. We need to feel good about ourselves to be able to trust our decisions and ideas. As we build our self-confidence, our ability to trust ourselves grows. Through our experience we build trust in ourselves, a kind of 'well I got myself this far so I must be doing ok' learning process. Our past experiences can serve to bolster our self-esteem. Whenever you feel you cannot trust yourself, go back through your life and see where you have been trust-worthy. What were you feeling at that time, how did you act, what did you base your decision on at that time? All these things can demonstrate to you that you can trust yourself. Acknowledge your successes and in this way we earn our own trust and life begins to feel less precarious.

The second 'who' that we learn to trust is our Self. As we tune into our intuition we can begin to act on it daily, the little stuff as well as the big life-changing decisions. Through this experience we build a trust in our Self, the guiding part of us. With each 'success' we become stronger in our Self-trust and life begins to feel more at ease. Again, it is a matter of practise, the old adage 'practise makes perfect' rings true as with all our spiritual practises. One thing that can help you become more trusting of your intuition is to journal your experiences. The act of writing our experiences embeds them deep within and you will recall them more readily. You build an inner database of your successes. Each experience of listening to our Self, and seeing the unfolding of our lives through guidance builds a level of trust that supports us on our journey.

So what is the 'what' we need to trust? I like to think of it as trusting the process. Some might say it isn't a 'what' but a 'who' – God. However, for me it is greater than what our limited minds think of as an entity, a greater power. It is God that is all-encompassing, God as a process of life unfolding. In fact, in this situation you could exchange the words God and life and it would be the same. You learn to trust in life. This life unfolds for each individual but is also a part of the whole of life unfolding. Life as in 'all that is'. If we can truly come to trust the process of our life and surrender our needs (something we will explore in the next chapter) then we will know in the deepest part of us that everything is as it should be.

Paulo Coelho's book, *The Alchemist*, illustrates this idea of trusting the process of life beautifully. In this story a Spanish shepherd goes in search of treasure beyond his dreams. His search takes him through many adventures and challenges and when he eventually finds his treasure it is in a place he would never have imagined. When he set out he had no idea where his life would lead but trusting the process of life brought him his goal. Had he not done so he would never have found either his treasure, his Soul mate or the enriching life experiences that taught him so much along the path.

All of us can look back through our lives and see how everything has a purpose. If we look through the victim's glasses it might be hard to discern the gifts, but if we look without judgement and with acceptance and honesty, we will see how everything brought us to where we need to be. You might not like where you are right now but it is leading you to your next lesson, to your highest truth. 'Life can only be understood backwards but must be lived forwards' is a truism. A few years ago I was complaining to a woman I had met on a course that lots of things had happened in my life that I wouldn't have necessarily chosen. She turned round to me and asked, "Do you like where you are right now?" I replied, "yes." Then she said "Well everything that has happened in your life has led you to here right now, therefore how can anything be wrong?" It was such a powerful moment and gave me the insight into the perfection of the process of life. With this understanding it was much easier to trust it.

Learning to Trust and Have Faith

We are taught to have trust and faith through our challenges. These may be smaller everyday occurrences, trying to deal with a child with measles when we are rushed with a deadline for example. Or they may be life-changing events like the death of a child. The common denominator is the challenge to our perspective, challenge to how we think something 'should' be. Amongst the many emotions will be the feeling of things not being right, not being fair. How useless we feel in that moment. Control is out the window, trust and faith are in, they are the only things that see us through. In these moments it is change that is the catalyst.

There are typical stages in our lives when we are challenged to trust something out of our control. These are not just when we are challenged through adversity; falling in love for the first time is a lesson in trust. Committing to a long-term relationship is another milestone. How about a parent trusting to let their child experience life, allowing them to play and fall over and scrape their knees, letting them go on the adventure holiday even though they might be feeling worried about it. Or the ultimate parental lesson, trusting that our children's decisions will work out to their advantage, that it is finally time to let them go and make their own mistakes, and successes. All of us will pass through our own lessons along the way. Each time we are being asked to learn to trust.

Early on in my spiritual search when I first visited the ashram in India I was given a card with the teaching 'Have Faith Everything is Alright'. This simple phrase struck me at the time and has been unfolding for me ever since. As we move along our path our interpretations of teachings are constantly upgraded in line with our understandings of truth.

When I first received this teaching I thought that it meant 'don't worry, everything is going to be fine'. However, it wasn't the 'fine' I was thinking about. I was still very much in need of everything being safe and in control. To me at the time that phrase meant not to worry, this is just a temporary glitch, 'normal service' will be resumed as soon as possible. How little did I know.

My life changed radically after that visit, and I gave up on 'normal service' years ago. For a while I was rather angry with the message on the card, what did it mean, 'everything is alright?' Not in my book it wasn't. I realise now that it was challenging me to change my needs and my addiction to an ordered world. It was hinting that life was fine, in fact life was perfect exactly as it was. A new post-India era was beginning for me, a time when spiritual principles were to become more than nice ideas. It was time to start living life spiritually.

[Cartoon: An angel sits behind a "COMPLAINTS" desk facing a person. Handwritten note: "NO, IT SAYS 'ALRIGHT' NOT 'SAFE'!"]

During my trip to Ireland soon after returning from India I got a hint of what this phrase might mean. I was feeling a bit lost. Not sure what my next step should be, so much of my life had been turned 180° and I felt uncertain and confused. Driving through the purple mountains in Kerry it was one of those beautiful, ethereal days that you sometimes get over there. I stopped the car and got out, a mist hung low amongst the hills and a quiet seemed to permeate the air. The purple mountains were earning their name that day and the scene felt other-worldly. I was literally stopped in my tracks by the perfection of the moment and it was an experience of everything being God, and everything, confusion and all, being all right.

These moments of perfection remind us to let go of our need for our world to be a certain way. By doing so our faith in the process does grow. We learn to have trust and faith. We begin to see that we can have preferences instead of addictions. It's always good to have intentions and goals as long as we can accept the outcome that our efforts bring. And trust that the outcome, whatever that may be, is exactly what is needed. An aid in this process is to take the personal out of situations. Often our initial reaction to any occurrence that involves us is to make it personal to ourselves. An alternative to this is to become the witness of what is happening. Rather than thinking 'this is happening to me', change your stance to 'this is happening and I can choose how I perceive it.'

Meditation is supportive in these times of challenges. As the world spins around us we get caught up in the hurricane of life, the what-ifs, the fear of consequences, the feeling of being out of control. If we can remember to hang onto the support of our spiritual practises at that moment we will handle it better. So often, we drop the things that would help us the most because we feel we have to take back control and *do* something. I know I have caught myself thinking 'I must do more' when I think that something is out of control. My ego plays the trump card of creating panic and driving me to take action, any action. My Self knows that this is the most important time to stay calm and focus on the inner play.

In a course I attended a Swami told a story of a woman who felt her life was spinning out of control. Her relationship had broken down, probably irrevocably, and she didn't know where she was going to live, how she was going to get over the heartbreak or how she was going to survive financially. Her mind was screaming for her to make something happen. Because of this need to 'do' she had argued that she did not have time for meditation anymore. She had to get on and sort out her life. The Swami replied that at times like these she should double her meditation. Our spiritual practises are not just something to enjoy when we have the time. Meditation will help us watch our minds and boost our resolve to trust no matter what. They are our life support.

One way we learn this trust is for us to learn through hindsight. Our journey contains the examples we need to see that, in fact there is a method to the madness called life. A client of mine was planning a career move. A lot of thought had been put into the plan, all the bases were covered, or so he thought. He had two interviews, either of which would have taken him onto the next level within his field. He interviewed for both positions but he was offered neither. He was crushed, couldn't understand what went wrong, what he had said or not said. He spent a large chunk of the next two weeks swinging between disappointment, anger and frustration. As we talked, I asked him what it was about the two new companies that drew him so much. I could understand the disappointment but he was overly upset, after all he was very capable and was sure to land the position he wanted sooner rather than later. He said that he really liked the two companies as they had a similar feel to the one where he was now. He liked his present company but it offered no promotional opportunity. With this in mind, we continued to refine his plan, adding the feel of the company he wanted to work in. He totally focused on what feeling he wanted, not on how he might achieve it, and trusted the process. He called me one day really excited. An opening had arisen totally unexpectedly in his present company and he had been offered the promotion. No move necessary.

By reviewing these types of experiences we can learn to trust that even when we are seemingly thwarted it is because life holds something else for us around the corner. We still need to put in the self-effort, remember the two wings of the bird, self-effort and grace – and then trust the process will bring us to exactly where we need to be. Take a look at your life. Where have you had these types of experiences? Has there been a time when if your life had followed the route you wanted then you would have lost out on something even better? Learn to trust from these moments.

It is useful to see these hindsight moments and keep them foremost in your mind when faced with a current challenge. As we learn to trust our own process called life, we can relax and become more present in what is happening now rather than worrying about the future. Remember, life is the Earth School in which we have our own individual lessons to learn. We might not like the outcome of some of the lessons, but they are necessary or we wouldn't be learning them. Nothing that happens is a mistake, look for the gift in each situation. This might be challenging and not immediately obvious, but however impossible it might seem at the time there is always a reason, a lesson, a gift. With this way of viewing our world we can learn that each one – a life-threatening illness, a break up of a relationship, losing the house we wanted to buy to someone else – gives us strength, endurance, patience and faith. And, if we choose to be open to the gift, each one brings us closer to the God within.

Faith and Prayer

Trust and faith are intertwined. My faithful old dictionary defines trust as 'belief in, reliance on, unquestioning faith in the reliability of a person'. So far so good. It defines faith as; 'confidence, trust, belief'. It also defines faith as 'belief in religious doctrines, the accepting of divine truth without actual proof'. This is where I think faith gets a bad name, the fear and balking that I mentioned earlier. Never once in my spiritual journey have I felt I was being asked by anyone or God to have blind faith. For me, faith is built by an inner experience. I believe in certain spiritual scriptures. I have faith in their veracity because of an inner knowing through living them. No outer intellectual proof, as in written guarantees, have been forthcoming, but plenty of inner Soul proof, experiences, have. Early on I remember reading 'accept nothing with blind faith, test everything with your heart'. Each crisis of faith ensures that we deepen our perceptions and anchors the truth within.

Prayer is a useful practise when confronted with a crisis, whether it be a crisis of faith or of a more material nature. Whenever I feel fear about a situation or making a decision I turn to prayer. Pray for strength, for faith, for the ability to trust the situation. Pray that you may learn the lesson with grace. And, if you are going to pray, make it a five-star prayer. Not an outcome prayer; a 'please make this happen'. Rather, make it a prayer about how it can empower you to be able to trust the process of life. And, know that each prayer is answered, you simply have to be open as to how.

Before I went to India I ran a retreat house in Devon. It was my first move out of the corporate world and I had prayed for an opportunity to change my life, make it more meaningful. I thought that the retreat house was the answer to my prayer. I bought a house, renovated it to be my home for many years to come and settled down into my new life. Eleven months later I had left. The true answer to my prayer actually lay in India. In an ancient Indian spirituality, a spiritual master, and a completely different way of understanding what life is about. Now, when I look back on that time in my life, I see that my prayer did get answered but it got answered in bits. The retreat house was 'safe' enough for me to leave the corporate world. It wasn't the answer to the prayer but simply a step towards the huge changes that were going to take place. Little did I think that my prayer would be answered in such a way.

As we learn to trust life and have faith in the process we will reap the benefits of them in our everyday lives. Fears will lessen their stranglehold over us. If we truly do trust that everything happens for a reason then we can stop worrying about the outcome and practise being ever more present in our lives. We will have equipoise in the face of adversity, a strong faith in our own destiny will give us strength through whatever life throws at us. Stress is lessened too. It becomes a pointer as to when we are not operating from a position of trust. We feel stressed because we feel out of control, overwhelmed, high-jacked by circumstances not always of our own making. As Mario Andretti, the F1 racing driver, was once quoted as saying, "If everything is under control you are going too slow!" Once we have trust in ourselves and in the bigger picture of our life then we can be present and let go of the worry that creates the stress.

Trust and faith beckon us to look for the positive in our lives. They help us create a reality through a good attitude to whatever is occurring. Trusting that all is for the best will encourage us to look for the gift in all situations, even when they really are not obvious. The biggest benefit of developing trust and faith is that it enriches our connection with Source. The God within and the connection with God in everyone and everything. By living our faith we constantly see the Grace in our life, the mystical elements that form an invisible thread that are our lives, our destiny, our journey back home. With this trust and faith we move closer to Remembering Perfection.

Tips

- We all need to learn to trust and have faith. As with intuition, start to build your self-esteem and confidence. Listen to your guidance within and acknowledge the times you do trust and have faith, bring them into the light and build on them. In this way you can learn to trust yourself and your Self.

- If you are having trouble trusting the process of life, seeing the perfection in the moment, step back from the personal. Instead of thinking 'this is happening to me', change your perspective to 'this is happening'.

- It is part of the spiritual path to doubt our beliefs, to experience the dark night of the Soul. Allow this crisis, relax into the fog, allow it to envelop you. Take time to explore what is there through meditation or contemplation. Know that you will emerge with a deeper connection to your inner life and God.

- As you go through your dark night find yourself a spiritual mentor or like-minded friend to travel the route with you. They won't have your answers but by listening to you they will validate the journey and your unique experience.

- Remember there is method in the madness and our desired outcome may not be the best. Trust the process, often there is more to it than meets the eye. To help you see this, ask yourself 'Where in my life have I wanted one thing that didn't happen only to find a better alternative around the corner?' Notice this, acknowledge it and use these experiences to build your faith in your life.

- If you feel you are being asked to have blind faith, take it to your heart, to your Soul, and ask, 'it this my truth?' Faith comes from within.

- Never forget prayer. Pray for strength, for faith, for trust. Prayers are always heard, however, the way they are answered may surprise you!

Contemplation

Give yourself at least half an hour for this contemplation. If you have a place within your home where you meditate use this space or if not just find somewhere quiet where you will not be disturbed. Have your journal or a notebook handy.

Before you start this contemplation, identify one idea or phrase that stood out for you in this chapter. For example, it may have made you wonder what your definition of trust and faith is. You now need to devise a question for you to contemplate. For example, it could be 'what does it mean to have faith?' Or 'how can I learn to trust?' Settle on whatever question feels right for you, something that will give you insight into the idea.

Get into a comfortable position and gently relax your body by taking some deep breaths. Breathe into any area of your body that holds tension and as you breathe out feel the tension flowing out with your breath. Once you feel relaxed bring your breathing back to your normal rhythm and simply focus on your breath for a few minutes. At this point invite Grace into your contemplation in whatever way seems appropriate for you. Now ask yourself the question you wish to contemplate. Ask it three times and then simply sit and see what comes to mind. If you find your mind wandering simply bring it back to the question. After sitting with the question for a while pick up your pen and begin to write. Let the answer flow, do not censor it, stop it or word-craft it. Simply allow your wisdom to emerge. Once you have finished sit quietly for a moment and acknowledge the wisdom and insight received.

CHAPTER TEN

Patience and Surrender

The final letting go and letting God.

So we've started to trust and have faith, what next? Patience and surrender. The final piece of the spiritual puzzle. By mastering these two virtues, we are more able to apply our spirituality in our everyday lives. But why do we need to have patience and surrender? Why can't we keep some semblance of control over what happens in our lives? The first answer that comes to mind is simply 'because!' That age-old answer that parents give their children when they are asked a difficult question. And in some ways it is the right answer because we actually need to surrender the need to know why. Why we have to do anything, why something happens, why we didn't get the life we thought we should have. All the 'why' questions.

In this chapter we will explore the mystery of surrender. We will look at what it is, and how we need to surrender our needs. We will investigate surrendering to our destiny and finally surrendering to our spiritual life. How we can totally let go and let God and the benefits of doing so. Whilst exploring patience we will see that it really is a virtue and begin to see what patience teaches us and how it is an evolutionary part of our journey. These two principles are not passive resignations but rather they are conscious actions with an energy that empowers our true spiritual life.

Patience is a Virtue

Over the years I have spoken to many people who are actively following a spiritual path. A common frustration I hear is that nothing happens fast enough and that they often feel it is one step forward and two steps back. As we have explored in earlier chapters, our lives in Earth School is where we learn whatever it is that will move us towards our final goal of enlightenment. Patience is one of the largest lessons. We are constantly challenged to let go of our own agenda and be present in whatever is unfolding in our lives at this moment.

I met a woman a few years ago who told a wonderful story to illustrate this lesson of patience. She was a dentist and had become inspired by the idea of a local organisation to create a children's mobile dental unit in the poorest county of upstate New York. She joined the team, envisioning that the unit would be set up within the year. Seven years later the first unit rolled out for the inaugural trip. She told this story not to complain about the delay but to show that there are always reasons for whatever happens. This seven-year wait held a crucial lesson for her. It was this: God's delay is not God's denial. She had to learn patience and she had to let go of her need for it to happen now, on her agenda. She also had to surrender her need to know why it hadn't happened as planned. Had the clinic been set up without the delay, she would never have imbibed this patience and surrendered so deeply.

We are often challenged to learn patience when we begin to get ahead of ourselves. When we see that something is moving, especially if it is something that we dearly want to have happen, we often forget that each experience has its own timing. We forget to be totally present and responsive and start to push the process ourselves. It is at moments like this that we stall, it begins to feel like we are pushing water uphill and a feeling of frustration often kicks in. This is us being told 'have patience', let go.

Patience also has a secondary and very important lesson in its arms. Endurance. I came across this idea a few years back in the infancy of my coaching business in Spain, when I was very impatient for it all to start to work. I wanted to know why things weren't happening to my plan, constantly questioned why, whenever it looked as though life was moving forward, it got blocked. I felt like I was playing the waiting game but didn't know the rules. I realised that there was obviously something for me to learn from this. The next day, I turned on the radio and tuned mid-way through a discussion about spirituality and how, as part of our spiritual evolution, we need to learn endurance. A light bulb went on. By being patient through the tough times we do learn to endure.

We learn to endure our disappointments, delays, failures and frustrations. This is not the endurance tied to the image of suffering. One definition of endurance is 'to bear with fortitude'. It is this elegant stance, a light and self-supportive way of being that patience teaches us. A realisation that we need to trust that our life's process is exactly as it is. A knowing that all we need to do is relax into life. This way we learn that these challenging situations truly teach us strength through the experience of endurance. With each test we begin to see that we are incrementally gaining strength in the face of adversity. Why do we need this strength? Because at some time in our life we will need to call upon this strength, this inner warrior, to face what life may throw at us.

I have a friend who was living through her second bout of cancer. We talked one day about how she was worried of the affect on her family, how unfair it was for them to be going through this with her. One of the things I asked her was how her husband had changed through the experience. What had he learnt through enduring this experience? She realised that this time round he was much stronger, he could handle it. She could also see that he had grown as an individual and as a Soul through his personal experience of her dis-ease. The patience we need to move through these types of challenges gives us huge reservoirs of strength that we would not have known were possible before. We are never sent a challenge too big for us, just as we are never given one too small. Our challenges, however painful, match us perfectly.

The strength that patience and endurance builds empowers us in many different areas of our life. It prepares us for the next big challenge: a break-up of a relationship, a death of a loved one, a change of financial circumstances. It also helps us in our daily life, the minor irritations of our day, the argument with our partner, a criticism of something at work, a head teacher calling to say our child has been misbehaving. If we have that level of solidity behind us we can deal with anything. Our state, both mental and emotional, will be much steadier. Our discipline in spiritual practises will be reinforced. That strength and discipline then become the cornerstone of our grounded spirituality.

Having and practising patience also helps us enjoy our lives. If we are impatient, we want something to happen now. We don't want to wait for the process to move forward step by step, we want the final outcome instantly. With this level of impatience we don't enjoy the journey, forgetting that it is equally as important as the goal. Doesn't sound very 'present moment' does it? It is more like we are living totally in the future. How many times have you not lived each experience, forgotten to practise patience along the way?

Organising any event can be a hotbed of impatience. For example, when organising a wedding it is easy to get stuck in the future. You know it's going to be a big day. You want it all perfect and spend hours making the plans, booking the venue, maybe writing your vows. Then there are the caterers, the menu, the bar, the band and the guest list. Oh, and don't forget the invites, the bridesmaids' presents, the best man's speech(!) the wedding supper. On and on it goes. Often you get so caught up in the plans for the big day, become impatient for it all to happen that you miss enjoying everything along the way. I remember speaking to a friend just after her wedding. She said that it all went by so fast that it was a blur. After so looking forward to the day all she could think of was what was supposed to happen next. Not only had she not been patient and enjoyed the planning she then forgot to enjoy the final product. An attitude of patience would have helped her be more present and experience whatever was happening throughout the whole time.

I caught myself forgetting to enjoy the journey recently. Living in Spain I need a lot of patience. In fact, I sometimes think that the only reason I moved here was to improve it. A while ago we bought some land with the intention to build a house. It has an old cortijo (farmhouse) on the land and we were told we would be able to refurbish it. You just need to register it and fill in a few forms, we were told. One-and-a-half years later we finally managed to complete the paperwork. Each time we thought we were ready to do so another obstacle came up. Problems buying the water rights, delays on the boundary agreement, changes in planning laws. With each delay I got angry and fed up and just wanted to wash my hands of the whole thing. However, another part of me knew this was just another test of patience. Not only patience with the system but it was also challenging me to live the whole process, the delays, the misinformation, the obstacles. I saw that I needed to be present, have patience and even enjoy this journey towards a beautiful home. Interestingly now with hindsight, that delay was a good thing because in the time it took to get everything ready to build, our life changed and it was no longer appropriate to live there. Had I been so impatient and somehow managed to push it all through, then we may not have been in such a good position as we are now. Funny how if we are patient life works out.

Patience is crucial as we live our spiritual path. It will constantly make us examine our faith. It will act as a catalyst for change, by being patient we can rein in the ego and its need to run the show. Each time we bring patience into the equation of our life it brings other gifts with it. We start to learn to be present, to relax into our life and trust it. If we have patience with each other we have the basis for loving each other unconditionally. We definitely need it when we create our reality, no deadlines allowed there. It really is a virtue and it also takes its twin, surrender, to make the whole package complete.

What is Surrender?

When I first talk about surrender with a new client they often feel that surrender is resignation, a giving up. This is a misunderstanding of spiritual surrender. Surrender is anything but passive. It is a conscious action, mentally, emotionally and energetically. If you are truly going to surrender, then all three aspects must have equal play. Remember the symbol of self-effort and Grace, the two wings of the bird? These elements still need to be present in everything we do. However, the next step is letting go of the attachment to the outcome of our efforts. In the ashram we offer voluntary service, called *seva* in Sanskrit. This is a giving back, a contribution to the Universe, a completion of the circle of giving and receiving. If you are visiting the ashram it may be for a couple of hours in the kitchen. If you are on long-term staff you offer *seva* for a full working day. Either way the energy behind it is the same. You put in the effort (one wing), Grace joins you (the other) and then you offer the fruits of your actions to God. You do not have the right to them. Rather you surrender them as a conscious action with the faith that the outcome is as it should be.

At the beginning, offering *seva* in the ashram with this in mind was a challenge for me. It felt as though I was unable to make something happen. Each time I tried to ensure a particular outcome I would be thwarted. I was constantly being pushed to let go of the outcome, let go of it being a certain way. Just put in the effort. One embarrassing experience of this was when I was asked to present some new principles to a group of teachers. These principles had been extracted from a larger document and we wanted people to grasp three particular ones that would then be incorporated into their courses. I devised a questionnaire that I thought would highlight the three principles and help everyone take them on board. I was very attached to them 'getting it' so of course it didn't work and the meeting did not go down the road I wanted. I tried to steer it back onto the course I wanted without success. At one point a very experienced and established teacher asked why I didn't just tell them what I wanted them to say and it would all be over much quicker. I was mortified. I felt like my manipulation had been exposed, and it had. I did, however, learn a very valuable lesson. I have to surrender the outcome, I have to offer my highest and let go.

Surrendering our needs is a big one. We will always be ruled by them until we do. Whenever I think of surrender I have the image of Bhagavan Nityananda, a revered Indian Saint who was a Guru to many. In photographs he is more often than not pictured with his hands wide open, almost extended backwards. This image to me embodies the idea of surrender, nothing is held, nothing is grasped, everything is released. Walking into the future, holding onto nothing. This feeling of constant letting go is surrender. A classic evening meditation is to see yourself burning all your worldly possessions. Each evening before you go to sleep imagine your possessions burning. Release them back to the Universe in the knowledge that should your life journey require them they will be there for you. As you energetically surrender your attachment to all your worldly possessions your inner freedom grows and with it the ability to surrender not only your worldly possessions but your attachments too.

As we progress on our spiritual journey we will be asked to surrender not only our needs, but our need to know why, how, where and when. A true sign of embodied spirituality is the ability to accept an outcome and not need to know why it happened. This is one of the things that hold us back from living in the present. The constant need to know why he left me, why didn't I get that job, why can't I have children, why didn't I get the visa to live in New Zealand. All these questions cripple us for the future. They act like a huge anchor dragging on the sea bottom. Surrender this need to know why and you will bring so much energy into the present time that things can start to move forward again.

Surrender of the 'how' is important too. The need to know how something is going to happen limits the miracles of the Universe. A few years ago we needed to get a new car. The one we had been borrowing for a while had to go back and we needed to replace it. In my mind we had to save up for a new one. However, each time we got some money in the bank another unexpected bill came along. It got nearer and near to the time when we needed the new car and I still held onto the thought that the only way, 'the how', was to save and buy one. In the end I realised that this simply wasn't going to happen and I realised I was being asked to surrender this 'how'. I had to let go of both how to get one and how to get around. I decided to drop the idea of a new car and to take up the offer from a friend of a scooter even though I hated them. A day later our phone rang and a friend said that she had someone in her office who wanted to give away a car. Were we interested? As soon as I had surrendered the 'how', I allowed the Universe to deliver the goods. Do not limit miracles.

Surrendering where and when is just as important too. If we insist on something happening at a particular place to our own timetable just think how many limitations that puts on our lives. Can you see any time in your life when you had these types of limitations, but once you let go something else came that fulfilled the need just as well? When we practise surrendering our needs, we are letting go to the bigger picture of our life. We are allowing that there is something larger than us, a reason and learning bigger than us, more than our minds can imagine. We can't fake this type of surrender, it has to occur on every level of our being, but once we get there, life does become an awfully big adventure.

How do we surrender these needs? What is the magic formula around surrender? Willingness and humility. A willingness to truly let go, not a fake willingness with conditions attached. Rather, this is a feeling of release within ourselves. For this willingness to be true, we need to find that place of humility within. This humility allows us to admit that we don't have all the answers, that we cannot know how to do this, that the bigger picture is greater than us. It is the humility that accepts that we are not yet perfect, that even though we may be a spark of divinity, we don't know it all the time. We need to be firm with our ego, who likes to have all the answers, and be willing to step back and not be in control. We have to cultivate a willingness to let our life unfold, to humbly surrender to God's plan, not ours. My will to Thy will.

Surrender to Destiny

In the Indian tradition of Kashmir Shavism, karma and destiny are major players in the illusion of life. Karma, the fruits of the seeds we sow, and our personal destiny are a key to understanding surrender. If it is true for you that we are a part of a universal play in which we each have our roles, then you have something to surrender into. As we have said, karma is all that happens, the only thing we can change is how we react to it. We can choose our attitude to what happens. If we know and believe we have a destiny to learn certain lessons, and experience certain events, then we can surrender into them. There is no reason to fight them. When I feel acute stress about a possible outcome that I might be dreading, if I can get my head, heart and Soul around the idea of surrender, in that moment something inside me releases. It is like a coil un-springing. I can rise above all the petty human fears and feel that everything is exactly as it should be. I do not need to know that the outcome will be 'safe'. Instead I have an inner knowing that the outcome just is.

This level of surrender can be applied to any everyday event whether it be positive or negative. We can surrender to the traffic jam as easily as we can surrender to a compliment. It is not that we surrender doggedly to the 'bad' things that happen. We also surrender to the 'good' things too. Surrender will bring whatever outcome is appropriate. A few years ago a woman told me a lovely story. She was a single parent without the means to go out and socialise very much. She therefore rarely met anyone new and her mother was always nagging her that she had to go out or she'd end up on her own. 'He's not going to walk up and knock on the door' her mother used to say with great regularity.

The woman, on the other hand, had a faith in destiny. She knew that if she was meant to be in another relationship, all she needed to do was surrender the limiting need to be in a relationship, and trust that her life would hold exactly what it needed for her. Then if a relationship came along, all well and good. If not, then at least she would have dealt with the fear of being alone, the feeling of need, of wanting to be taken care of and many other issues besides. She lived this surrender for a while and lo and behold, one day a fantastic man knocked on her door, literally. The rest is history!

The key here was she didn't surrender tactically so that she could meet someone, she surrendered full stop. Not: I'll surrender X if you give me Y. She worked with herself, knowing what was blocking her from becoming whole. The relationship that came was simply the next step for her. It was a necessary part of her life, her lessons, or it wouldn't have come. Now, that's complete surrender.

Surrender to our Spiritual Life

At some point on our spiritual path we need to surrender into it. If life is a spiritual journey there comes a moment when we need to let God drive the car. At the beginning we generally have a tendency to compartmentalise our life. Spirituality is one of the sections and it probably fights for time in the schedule along with social life, business, family and kids if you have them. As we move on, it begins to gain importance as we see its value, the benefits living your spirituality brings. I loved a comment a friend made years ago when we went to a meditation centre for the first time. Someone asked him if he would be coming back next week and he automatically answered, "yes if I'm not doing anything else." It was a get-out clause answer. To give him his due, he caught it straight away and said, "of course I'm coming, why would I want to do anything else?" This was the beginning of the surrender to the spiritual path. These are moments we start to notice how our ego is trying to deflect us.

Surrender at this level can happen in stages too. Each new opportunity to surrender takes us deeper. I can think of two very distinct times for myself. The first one happened during my visit to the ashram in India. It was the first time I had ever been to an ashram and I was very new to Indian philosophy. I could feel an internal struggle going on inside me. Part of me knew that this was a turning point moment; I had resigned my job to go there. Another part of me was fighting hard, trying to hold onto the old, safe life. It was fighting so hard that two weeks into the visit I decided that I had to leave and I had to leave now. With hindsight I realise that my ego knew that if I didn't escape now there was no turning back. Part of me knew that my life would never be the same again, I was on the verge of a life-changing experience. The spiritual teachings presented in the ashram resonated with a part of me deep within. The atmosphere permeated my being and I knew I had started the journey home. My ego wanted out – now. I rang the airline in Bombay (no mean feat 12 years ago) only to be told that all flights were full for the next three months. I was furious and by now desperate to leave the ashram. At no point did it occur to me that I could have simply walked out of the gates, in my mind I had to get out of the country.

I was still ranting and raving a couple of hours later when a friend turned round and said, "You are being asked to give 90 days of your life to God, is that so much?" This stopped me in my tracks. I literally walked straight to the reception and booked for another three months. This was the moment of surrender, of taking a deep breath and allowing my life to change and unfold in the way my Soul was so longing for. The postscript to that experience was that a few weeks later I called the airline again to rebook my flight home after my stay. I said I knew that they were fully booked for three months but could they add me to the standby list for 8 weeks from then. A surprised voice replied, "What do you mean we are fully booked, I can get you on a flight tomorrow." Sometimes we just have to surrender to our spiritual path.

The second opportunity for spiritual surrender came four years later. I had recently moved to the ashram in the USA. Still in a period of adjustment I was grappling with the implications of applying spirituality in everything and feeling a huge resistance to what felt to me like a surrender of me. One night I had a very powerful dream in which I was driving a large refrigerated lorry to a specific destination but I kept on taking diversions and stopping along the way for all sorts of strange reasons. Anything I could think of to delay the inevitable I did. I'd look at the map and find different routes that went to lovely holiday places instead of taking the direct route. It was a very higgledy-piggledy journey. At one point I realised that if I didn't get going, if I didn't take whatever was inside this lorry to the destination then it would be too late. The goods would be ruined. It was at that point in the dream that I started to head towards my destination. When I woke I felt very disturbed by the dream, I knew deep inside that I was being asked a question. I went to meditate and asked to be given a clue as to what the question was. What came to me was that I was being asked to commit to my path, surrender to my process. Stop taking detours and learn to live with a growing awareness and surrender my ego. As this came to me the tears began to flow and I dropped into my heart, and there, etched as though in stone, were the words 'Whatever it takes'.

Surrender happens for us all in our individual ways. You don't need to be living in an ashram for it to occur. Take a look back through your experiences and ask yourself where you have been asked to surrender. Maybe you've had to surrender a need, whether it be a material need or simply the need to know why something happened. Or perhaps you're learning to surrender to your destiny, see that your karma is unfolding exactly as it should be. You also might have had the experience of surrendering to your spirituality, allowing it to be the leading light in your life.

As we move through our spiritual life we meet these milestones along the way. Beginning to trust and have faith, we also surrender in increments. Sometimes these are pivotal moments, some slip by nearly unnoticed. None are minor. As our ego becomes purer we surrender our personal agenda to our Soul's agenda. We practise the patience necessary for us to learn the lessons along the way and we begin to live in an awareness of God. We know that we are on the right path for us, that love operates throughout our lives and we give back through that love and enjoy God's play. And, as we rise above the mundane and live our surrender, we Remember Perfection.

Tips

- If you feel that you are being stalled, if it begins to feel like you are pushing water uphill and a feeling of frustration is kicking in remember that this is you being told to 'have patience', let go. If something isn't happening to your timetable, ask yourself, is this God's denial or God's delay?

- When you feel like you are enduring something, that patience is showing you a lesson, notice what strength you are learning through this endurance. How will this serve you in the future? Can you be grateful for it?

- If you are feeling impatient take a breath, bring yourself back to the present moment. Being present helps you see your impatience and gives you the moment of choice to let it go.

- To practise surrender; each time you embark on a new task offer up the outcome to God. Surrender the fruit of your action to God. Be the hands of God, not the controller.

- Practise the evening meditation of releasing your worldly possessions. Each evening before you go to sleep imagine your possessions burning. Release them back to the Universe in the knowledge that should your life journey require them they will be there for you. This energetic surrender helps you have an attitude of surrender in your everyday life.

- If you find yourself at odds with a situation in your life ask yourself, 'How humble am I right now?' 'How willing am I to surrender this situation?'

- If you feel that your spiritual practise is dry, not fruitful, even boring, answer this question honestly: 'How surrendered am I to my spiritual path, have I really invited God in to drive the car?'

Contemplation

Give yourself at least half an hour for this contemplation. If you have a place within your home where you meditate use this space or if not just find somewhere quiet where you will not be disturbed. Have your journal or a notebook handy.

Before you start this contemplation identify one idea or phrase that stood out for you in this chapter. For example, learning endurance through patience may have stood out for you. Or, surrendering your need to know why something happened. Whatever it was, you now need to devise a question for you to contemplate. For example, it could be 'how can I be more patient?' Or 'how can I let go of the need to know why something happens?' Settle on whatever question feels right for you, something that will give you insight into the idea.

Get into a comfortable position and gently relax your body by taking some deep breaths. Breathe into any area of your body that holds tension and as you breathe out feel the tension flowing out with your breath. Once you are relaxed bring your breathing back to your normal rhythm and simply focus on your breath for a few minutes. At this point invite Grace into your contemplation in whatever way seems appropriate for you. Now ask yourself the question you wish to contemplate. Ask it three times and then simply sit and see what comes to mind. If you find your mind wandering simply bring it back to the question. After sitting with the question for a while pick up your pen and begin to write. Let the answer flow, do not censor it, stop it or word-craft it. Simply allow your wisdom to emerge. Once you have finished sit quietly for a moment and acknowledge the wisdom and insight received.

CHAPTER ELEVEN

What Now?

An idea is just that until you add the magic ingredient of commitment.

So now what? You've read through to the end of the book. Maybe you liked certain principles better than others, agreed with some things, disagreed with others. Perhaps what you read inspired you, made you excited with the possibilities, or maybe you felt frustrated, or even angry. Whatever your reaction, you now have two choices. Find a nice safe place for the book on your bookshelf, add it to the others that you have and never consider it again. Or, do something with it.

I recommend the second option. This book is about applied spirituality. The key word here is application. Until you use this information your life will not change. They may be nice ideas, but they will stay ideas until you incorporate them into your life. It is not for nothing that spiritual practises are called practises. Two phrases come to mind: practise makes perfect, and practise what you preach. By adding a spiritual practise to your life then you will begin, or enrich, your Soul's journey home.

One piece of invaluable advice I received early on in my spiritual life was to choose one practise. As you can see from this book there are many we can do, but if we try to do them all it is a set-up for failure. Imagine when we break the pack on the first shot on a pool table. The balls scatter and only if we are very lucky does one go down the hole. However, when we focus on one ball and try to pot it in a particular hole we have a much greater chance of success. Spiritual practises are just like this. By focusing on one aspect, one principle, we have a far greater chance of being successful and making the practise an ingrained part of our lives. Unless we are living a cloistered monastic life we all have everyday responsibilities to attend to. Be it a job, family, child or elderly care, voluntary work, the list is endless. We all have calls on our time and whether we class these as work or play they all need to be juggled so that life happens. If you try to add five new spiritual practises at once you might last a few days, but in the end they will all fall by the wayside.

The trick is to take one. Just one. As you read this book there was probably one or a couple of chapters that stood out for you. Again – 'if it comes to your attention, give it your attention'. What grabbed your attention? What one principle appeals to you? What can you envision adding to your life, something that will have sticking power? To help yourself, make sure it is attainable. You want to stretch, but give yourself a winning hand. Remember my test of seeing God in Spanish drivers? Start somewhere obvious; stack the cards in your favour. It doesn't actually matter which one it is, intention is incredibly powerful and practising one aspect will gradually draw the other principles into your life too.

For example, if you choose to practise gratitude you will probably find yourself becoming more present. Practising gratitude will help you notice the things that are happening in your life. Firstly, you may only remember to make a list of them at night, but as you gradually become accustomed to seeing the things you are grateful for, you will begin to see them as and when they happen. In other words, you will become more present. As you notice what happens throughout your day it will become natural for you to see how you can actually create your own reality. By being present, you will begin to notice the 'co-incidences' of when you thought about something and it happening. These occurrences will give you the faith to follow your intuition, will empower you to choose your attitude, and give you the self-confidence to be more real within your world. By being real, you will then begin to see God in each other. And so the process evolves.

Likewise, by practising unconditional love, you will begin to see God in each other, seeing the love present in everything. This love will show you a world without so much judgement, a world where you can choose your attitude in relationship with others. You will learn to have faith and trust life and start to take responsibility for your reality. This change in attitude will empower you to live your life being totally real to yourself. In turn, you will be challenged and the principle of patience will then come into play. Faith will be strengthened in these times and you will learn the ultimate principle of surrender, to yourself, to your spiritual life, to God.

The interconnectedness of the Universe is the same in all aspects. It is not just the oneness of us as Souls. Your intention to apply spiritual principles in your life, whichever one you start with, will bring them all into play eventually. It is like a spiral path, a Universe that has no end or beginning, simply step into it wherever you feel drawn and know that you will walk it all in your own time. For each of us the timing of our journey is unique. We each have our own things to learn and therefore our lessons are individual to us. Our lifetimes are our Earth School and we never stop learning and growing back into ourselves until we reach the final attainment of oneness, enlightenment, that moment when all separation is gone. Our desire for this state will determine how much self-effort we put into living our spirituality. Remember the two wings of the bird? Our self-effort is met with Grace, without the two wings there is no forward progress, only ever-decreasing circles.

Once you have decided where to start the next choice is the practical. The how. How will you add this principle to your life? What format might it take? How can you remember each day? Maybe set aside a time of the day to focus on your chosen principle. By setting aside a time, you are carving out a small part of the day and creating a habit, a good one. For example, you might start the day with a ritual of remembrance. It could be part of a meditation or maybe it is a visualisation you revel in for five minutes before your day starts. If you were choosing to practise gratitude you might repeat 'I am grateful for all events in my life.' You can also have something written, or a picture, some visual reminder somewhere that you can review each morning. Whatever it is, make it a daily ritual.

At the end of the day acknowledge how you did. What was it about practising that principle that made you feel good, what positive outcomes did it have? You can also review what it was that made you fall down, or forget the principle. How might you approach a similar situation differently? It doesn't matter that you forgot or didn't handle a situation as you would want to. All that matters is that you acknowledge where improvement is possible and thank yourself for trying. We all know that when you fall off a horse you have to get back on straight away. Spirituality is that horse. You will fall off and sometimes you might lie on the ground for quite a while, perhaps with a little spiritual concussion. However, eventually you will come to and get back on the horse. At that point it's always useful to ask yourself the question, 'What did I learn from that experience?' By doing so, you start to create a new awareness of yourself and your patterns of behaviour and then you can choose to change them. And remember there is no such thing as failure, only feedback, learn from everything. After a while you will begin to catch yourself every time you trip back to your old habits. At this point you can widen the net, perhaps apply the principle at work as well as at home, or even add another and let the greater awareness trickle through all areas of your life.

And don't forget you are never alone on the journey. Sometimes, especially when we are feeling challenged, when we feel we are in the dark night of the Soul we can feel very alone, abandoned, separate. In truth, these are the times when God is the nearest, we are just so caught up in our worldly drama we cannot see or hear. I know nowadays that when I recognise that feeling, I am being challenged to surrender to what is happening. To bring God closer, meditate more, pray more, and practise gratitude more. As you walk this path remember to pray for strength, help and guidance, not just in the times of challenge but also make it part of your daily ritual. It doesn't have to be long and involved, a heartfelt prayer takes but a second. All these supports are available to you so use them.

The magic ingredient in this mix is commitment.

A famous quote by Bill Murray of the Scottish Himalayan Expedition says:

> *"Until one is committed there is hesitancy the chance to draw back, always ineffectiveness.*
> *Concerning all acts of initiative (and creation) there is one elementary truth, the ignorance of which kills countless ideas and splendid plans: the moment one definitely commits oneself, then Providence moves too. All sorts of things occur to help one that would otherwise not have occurred.*
> *A whole stream of events issues from the decision, raising in one's favour all manner of unforeseen incidents and meetings and material assistance, which no man could have dreamed would have come his way."*

This was one of the first 'spiritual' quotes I read, soon after that first personal growth course that started my search. It struck me deeply then and I have experienced it to be true. As soon as I committed to a spiritual path, my life changed, opportunities came my way and great support to help me materialised. The energy of commitment is a magnet of great power.

Without commitment anything is just a nice idea. It is something that we like, that we might take up in the future, rather similar to liking amateur dramatics but never quite getting around to joining the local society. Commitment takes guts, a standing up and saying, 'I want this to change and I am ready to do what it takes'. I want to experience these principles at work in my life. I will practise gratitude, learn to listen to my intuition, surrender my needs everyday. I will set aside half an hour to sit quietly with my Self and become aware of the divinity in me and my life. Not only will Providence move to support your commitment, you will also feel empowered by your attitude of commitment. Think back to when you were truly committed to something, when you made something happen in your life. Didn't you feel good about yourself? Didn't you go up in your own estimation and in your self-esteem? You will become a more dynamic, innovative person once you have made the commitment to yourself.

To help yourself with your commitment, communicate it to others close to you. You cannot make these changes in a vacuum, so engage others who will support you. Ensure these are the people who truly wish you to follow your heart's desire. We all have people in our lives who say they wish to support us, but are actually the downers. They will give us an excuse just as things get challenging; they will question why we wish to change, all the while saying they support us. Us changing means that they may have to change in relationship to us. They have a vested interest in us staying the same, they are the silent saboteurs, stay clear of them. Also it is good to have someone to support you, to check in with and encourage you to keep going. It is nice to have someone who helps you integrate this new aspect of you into your everyday life. A spiritual mentor, coach or friend as we mentioned before, can help validate your experience simply by witnessing you on the path.

Spiritual principles are not separate from your life but an integral part and so need to be at the centre, part of every aspect of what you do. For this to happen you need as many reminders as possible. As well as talking about it to others and enlisting their support, visual aids are also helpful for this. Create a spiritual treasure map; add pictures that represent how you'd like to be in your life. Take a look at the tips at the end of each chapter and maybe copy them out and stick them on too. Write on any inspirational quotes you find. Have your map somewhere very visible, and keep adding to it when you find something that fits. Change the positioning every couple of days or you will start to screen it out, it will just become part of the wallpaper. That may sound odd but I heard story about a woman who created a huge **treasure** map as her inspiration and when she moved house she **left** it behind. She didn't even see it any more and only realised she hadn't moved it with her when a friend asked where it was. So use as many means of support that resonate with you and make them visible daily.

As you work with the principles, daily acknowledge your progress, see the benefits to what you are bringing into your life. Journaling can help here. So often in our busy lives we forget just how far we've come. It is useful to have a written record of our journey, not only so you can look back and see the progress, but also so you can truly acknowledge it. Writing things down helps you get clear on what you have learnt too. Remember that if you fall down on your commitment do not beat yourself up. We are human, we do have our weaknesses and this is a journey towards wholeness. Every journey has its hiccups. The only thing you have to do when you realise you've missed the path is re-commit and step back on. As this commitment deepens and you integrate the spiritual into the worldly, you feel the difference in your mental state. You will begin to relax into your life in the Earth School. You will experience the positive side of being able to step back and maybe take life a little less personally.

The final stage of commitment is this:

Do it.

Do it now.

Choose what you wish to start with. Decide how and when and what will it look like in your life. And start – Today.

Why?

Why do it?

Well in my experience we yearn for the spiritual in our life because the world is only in a half-light without it. Day after day the world revolves around the sun and we feel we are on the treadmill of life. Things happen that we have no reason for, can see no sense in. Only when you add the spiritual, the greater purpose, the bigger picture to the equation does the light truly shine. It is the difference between a grey, cloudy, rainy day and blue skies and sunshine with a white sand beach thrown in. It is the difference between a small, polite smile and huge, belly clutching, convulsive laughter. It is the difference between a kiss on the cheek from an acquaintance and a passionate kiss from a lover. God is the ultimate lover, feeling oneness with God is bliss. As you reach that point, however fleeting or long it might be, you know that you never, ever, wish to go back. A feeling of such joy is beyond words. Millions of people around the world have devoted their lives to attaining the wordless. Those who achieve it are the living proof that it is real and available to us all. To begin this journey is the one true adventure with the ultimate prize.

That's why.

To support you in using the ideas and tips in this book I am happy to offer you some complimentary downloads from the website. Please visit www.rememberingperfection.com to download them.

Bibliography

From the Heart of Gentle Brother	Bartholomew
The Field	Lynne McTaggart
Time to Think	Nancy Kline
Loving What Is	Byron Katie
Sacred Contracts	Caroline Myss
The Path to Love	Deepak Chopra
Conversations with God books	Neale Donald Walsh
The Heart of Meditation	Swami Durgananada
Ask and it is Given	Esther & Jerry Hicks
Ignorance	Milan Kundera
The Prophet	Kahlil Gibran
What's on my Mind?	Swami Anantananda
The Alchemist	Paulo Coelho
Stranger in Paradise	Julie Chimes

Additional recommendations

The Astonishing Power of Emotions	Esther & Jerry Hicks
Where are you Going?	Swami Muktananda
Courage and Contentment	Swami Chidvilisananda
The Power of Now	Eckhart Tolle

A New Earth	Eckhart Tolle
A Return to Love	Marianne Williamson
Presence	Senge, Scharmer, Jaworski, Flowers
Synchronicity	Joseph Jaworski
7 Habits of Highly Effective People	Stephen Covey
Finding Your Own North Star	Martha Beck
Feel the Fear and Do it Anyway	Susan Jeffers
Everyday Grace	Marianne Williamson
When Things Fall Apart	Pema Chödrön
The Artists Way	Julia Cameron
Invisible Acts of Power	Caroline Myss
Quantum Healing	Deepak Chopra
Illusions	Richard Bach
Turning Passions into Profits	Christopher Howard
Death is an Illusion	Else Byskov
Advanced Energy Anatomy, CD	Caroline Myss
Spiritual Madness, CD	Caroline Myss
The Secret behind The Secret DVD	Esther & Jerry Hicks
What the Bleep Do We Know? DVD	Matlin, Hendrix, Bowie
www.jessicamcgregorjohnson.com	My personal website
www.abraham-hicks.com The Teachings of Abraham	Esther & Jerry Hicks
www.tut.com Daily notes from The Universe	Mike Dooley
www.syda.org	SYDA Foundation
www.myss.com	Caroline Myss

Glossary

Affirmation

A positive, present tense statement stating a desired outcome. Affirmations help unearth limiting beliefs and the saboteur, as well as being one of the tools for changing the negative beliefs held around personal wishes.

Ashram

A spiritual retreat site where people engage in spiritual practises under the guidance of a Spiritual Master. The focus of an ashram is often a daily schedule of events which can include chanting, meditation, and *seva* as well as a variety of courses for people to deepen their understanding and experience.

Blessings

A prayer of love bestowed upon another.

Chakras

The seven energy centres found within the subtle energy body that relate to the wellbeing of different aspects of our physical, emotional and spiritual self.

Contemplation

A practise of going within and asking for guidance from our higher Self.

Destiny

Our individual life path according to our personal karma. We live our destiny which is governed by the life lessons we need this time round.

Duality

See separateness.

Earth School

A term to describe our personal world in a way that helps us remember that we are here for a purpose, that we have incarnated to learn specific life lessons.

Ego

The limited sense of 'I' that identifies with the body, mind and emotions and which creates the feeling of duality, e.g. I am beautiful, I am dumb, I am happy.

Enlightenment

The ultimate goal on the spiritual path, when one lives in the constant of awareness of the God within and the oneness of everything.

Fire Ceremony

An ancient fire ritual in which offerings of ghee, wood etc are offered to the fire as a token of gratitude. Also called a Yajña.

Fire Of Yoga

The purification process that occurs as you practise yoga. This is the purification of the ego, that part of us that keeps the veil of separation in place.

God's Play/Lila

In the Shavite tradition the creation of all is often described as God's Play, the Divine Play or Lila.

Grace
The divine energy of the Universe. This supports us in our lives to remember our oneness, and overcome the suffering that our identification of duality gives us.

Guru
A spiritual master who has attained enlightenment and can guide others on their spiritual journey.

Illusion
The illusion of the world is the limiting belief that this dimension is all there is. To be caught in the illusion is to be caught in Maya.

Intention
A clear vision of what you wish to happen, empowered with a belief in its possibility accompanied by a tangible feeling of it created on an energetic level.

Karma
The destiny of a person created by past actions. Karma is not good or bad, it simply is the result of previous occurrences. It can be said to be everything that happens in life.

Kashmir Shavism
A part of Shavite philosophy that teaches the non-duality of the Universe, that everything is one with God, the Divine.

Life Purpose
A higher, more meaningful focus in life, in line with our destiny, which when lived brings fulfilment.

Limiting Belief or Decision
Beliefs or decisions we have made unconsciously, derived from the meaning we gave to an experience in our life, that limit our way of thinking and stop us living to the full.

Maya
An ancient scriptural term for the veil which hides our oneness with God.

Medical Intuitive
A person who can intuitively diagnose illness within another.

Meditation
A practise of being quiet and going within to help become more aware. Often done with the mind focusing on the breath.

Oneness
The experience that there is no difference between all things in the Universe, everything is one with God, everything is God.

Patterns Of Behaviour
Actions that are recurring, often unconsciously, that can be negative. Spiritual practises help us notice these patterns and change them.

Reality
The truth of a situation in a moment unrelated to what we may be thinking about it.

Reincarnation
The belief that we live successive lives, being reborn both as man and woman.

Sanskrit

The ancient language of the Indian Scriptures.

Sannyasin

A person who has taken the vows of monkhood in which he/she renounces the world and dedicates their life to the goal of enlightenment.

Self/Soul

The unchanging, pure, non-egoic aspect of us. The Self is often likened to the drop of rain which is part of the ocean. Even when that drop is in cloud form its source was the ocean and it will eventually return to the ocean.

Separateness/Duality

The egoic belief that we are all separate beings rather than a part of the wholeness of the Divine.

Seva

Selfless service, work offered to God without attachment to the outcome. In ashrams *seva* is a spiritual practise that helps people become aware of their egoic tendencies especially when interacting with others.

Shakti

A divine spiritual power which according to Kashmir Shavism is the creative power of the Universe.

Source

Another word for God, Universe, Divinity or Providence

Spiritual Practise

A regular action i.e. meditation, contemplation, that is used to help build an awareness of personal spirituality, purify the mind and integrate spiritual and everyday life.

Spiritual Principles

Different aspects of spirituality such as seeing God in each other, practising gratitude or being real that when lived aid us towards liberation.

Swami

A title of respect for a sannyasin or monk.

Tribal Mind

A term used to describe the collective consciousness of a particular group of people. i.e. the typical thinking within a peer group of teenage girls or within a family.

Universe

Another word for God, Divinity, Source or Providence.

Yoga (*lit Union*)

A state of Oneness with the divine, also the spiritual practises and disciplines that help us reach that state of oneness. There are many types of yoga, the best known Hatha Yoga, a physical discipline. Other yogas include: Bhakti Yoga, the yoga of devotion, Karma Yoga, the yoga of action and Raja Yoga, the yoga of the mind, of study and contemplation.

About the Author

Jessica lives in Southern Spain and works internationally as a life fulfilment coach, empowering people to move past old limitations and create success in any area of their life. There is a strong spiritual aspect to the way she works, as she truly believes that we are all connected and that there is far more than meets the eye when it comes to who we are as energetic beings. Bringing that aspect to her work means that she addresses the deeper issues that some people hold and moves her clients towards a place of wholeness, which is where fulfilment lies.

Through the work, her clients learn the ability to be a positive influence in their own lives, changing the way they communicate both with themselves and others, and they go on to produce the big changes they wish for in their lives.

If you would be interested in exploring working with Jessica please do get in touch through her website: www.jessicamcgregorjohnson.com

Printed in the United Kingdom
by Lightning Source UK Ltd.
134849UK00002B/58-150/P